GREAT RAILWAY
BATTLES

GREAT RAILWAY BATTLES

Dramatic conflicts
of the early railway years

Geoffrey Body

Silver Link Publishing Ltd

© Geoffrey Body 1994

First published in August 1994

British Library Cataloguing in Publication Data

A catalogue record for this book is available from the British Library

ISBN 1 85794 033 4

Silver Link Publishing Ltd
Unit 5
Home Farm Close
Church Street
Wadenhoe
Peterborough PE8 5TE
Tel/fax 0832 720440

Printed and bound in Great Britain

CONTENTS

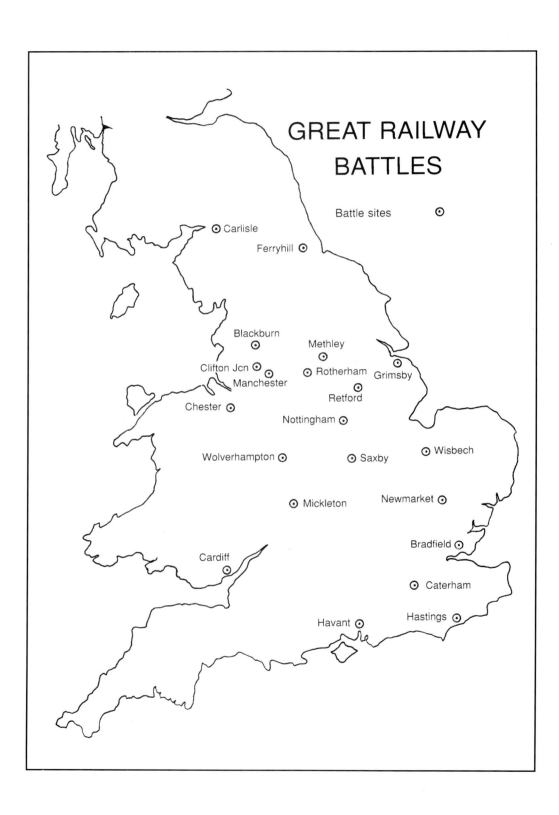

INTRODUCTION AND ACKNOWLEDGEMENTS

The railway system was born in an era that saw Great Britain experiencing change at an incredible rate. Within the space of a century the economic and social structure of the country altered from its centuries-old farming base to a new society dominated by the dark Satanic mills of industry and the coal, iron and water that fed them. The effect on the nation and its people was dramatic. The rich survived, the enterprising prospered and the workforce slowly benefited from the pain of the rapid and extensive alterations in their working and living environment.

As with most periods of rapid change, the process was erratic and often ill-disciplined. Led by invention and innovation, the pace became self-accelerating with no time for tidying up before the next excitement came along. Even the legislature slowly relinquished its traditional conservatism for a more adventurous outlook and, imperceptibly, attitudes moved towards a commercial philosophy characterised by a healthy regard for profit and a fairly laissez-faire approach to the means of its achievement.

Prior to the dawn of the railway era the transport scene had already witnessed road carriers and stage coach operators crippled by the coming of the canals. In their turn the latter were to face the competition of railways. At the same time, as the scope and pace of change quickened, so the monetary stakes were being raised by the increasingly higher investment required by new schemes. In this climate landowners and entrepreneurs watched the changing commercial world with acute self-interest, and the ordinary folk wondered anxiously whether new schemes would bring new jobs or merely threaten old ones.

Arising from the sheer rate and extent of change from about 1740 onwards there was just not enough time for the political and legislative machinery to keep pace. Quite apart from the increasing complexity of the wider national and international affairs, each fresh commercial activity demanded new legislation for its gestation and control, and the finer points of business dealing and practice rarely got detailed attention. More often was it expedient to use old legislation for new circumstances, and to produce general Acts that would simplify the Parliamentary workload at the same time as curbing the worst risks of excesses. The overall climate was thus one of rapid change involving increasing investment and technological development, but subject, in the main, only to basic legislation constructed with little precedent or real understanding.

In these circumstances of great change and relatively little control, the sheer pace of events led the enterprising to act first and justify afterwards. The stakes were too high for constant reference to precedent or conventional morality, and it is hardly surprising that the niceties were forgotten from time to time. Applied to the initial growth period of Britain's railway system, this factor produced a number of cases of rowdy and rumbustious confrontation. Today the thought of crowds of labourers brought in to solve a dispute by brandishing pick-axe handles and setting about their opponents' host seems mildly bizarre, but yesterday's circumstances were vastly different. The events, with their extrovert characters and colourful incidents, may now seem a bit larger than life, but they make excellent reading and cast a light on the moral and other standards of the day, which often gets lost in the painting of wider literary canvasses.

So far as sources are concerned, most of the standard railway histories make reference to the incidents described in this book, but the principal repositories of detailed information are the local newspapers of the areas concerned. Several of the 'battles' have featured in the pages of *The Times*, some in the *Illustrated London News* and others in the learned pages of the R&CHS *Journal*, and in the works of such bodies as the Cambridgeshire Antiquarian Society, the Lancashire & Cheshire Antiquarian Society and the Durham County and Havant local history groups. In addition to the articles in *The Railway Magazine* and such early publications as the *Railway & Travel Monthly* and *Herapath's Journal*, information can also be found in the pages of the *Hampshire Magazine*, the *East Anglian Magazine*, *The Builder* and *The Portsmouth Papers*. Oakwood Press volumes on the Caterham, Taff Vale, Rhymney, East Lancashire and Oxford, Worcester & Wolverhampton railways all contribute to the picture, with especially detailed data on South Wales appearing in that publisher's 1987 work *The Cardiff Railway* by Eric R. Mountford. Other booklets of special relevance include *The Byers Green Branch* by R. S. Abbey, *The Mistley, Thorpe & Walton Railway* by Thomas B. Peacock, and the author's early work on the East Anglian Railway. Of special background relevance to Chapters 16 to 18 are the exchanged letters between the South Eastern and the London, Brighton & South Coast railways.

It has to be said that some of the newspapers of the last century were fallible in their facts and as anxious as some of their modern contemporaries to dramatise events to increase their news value. However, such colouring as contributes without distortion has been left in these accounts in the belief that it adds to their reality; not to the detriment of historical truth, of course, but hopefully to the advantage of readability and enjoyment.

Apart from the *Illustrated London News*, from which the vivid scene in Chapter 9 is culled, there are virtually no real sources of illustrations for the period covered in the pages that follow. To remedy this an effort has been made to bring the locality to life by including more maps and diagrams than average, with the main photographic coverage devoted to the location as it is now. Tracking down the exact spot where a specific incident occurred has not always been easy, but the detective work involved has often added a spice to and understanding of the event that readers may wish to experience for themselves. All illustrations are from the author's collection unless otherwise shown. The maps are designed to be self-explanatory, but it should be noted that broken lines normally indicate a railway not open at the period portrayed.

Especial thanks are due to Peter Townsend and Will Adams at Silver Link Publishing for their faith in and help with this project; to Ian and Richard Body for the maps, advice and initial research; to my wife for reading the finished typescript; to Mrs Ann Wilson at the Ken Hoole Study Centre; and to Brion Purdy, Principal Library Manager, East Sussex County Council. Also to the staff at the Public Record Office, Kew; the Leicester Record Office & Local Study Centre; the Croydon Local Studies Library; and the Wisbech & Fenland Museum. This book could not have been prepared without the generous and enthusiastic contribution of the staff of the local study centres and reference libraries at Blackburn, Bristol, Cambridge, Cardiff, Carlisle, Chester, Colchester, Darlington, Doncaster, Grimsby, Hastings, Manchester, Newport, Nottingham, Oakham, Portsmouth, Wolverhampton and York. To all of them my grateful thanks.

1
THE TRIBULATIONS BEGIN

'Stand aside, or I shoot.' These words, or their equivalent, were used by Charles Frow, a surveyor hailing from Thorpe in Lincolnshire, in a moment of great frustration and anger. They were addressed to a gamekeeper in the Stapleford Park home of Lord and Lady Harborough during an incident in the middle years of the last century. The occasion was one of the early route surveys being conducted on behalf of the Midland Railway, in this case for the purpose of preparing plans for a line of railway from Syston to Peterborough.

'Shoot away!' The response to Frow's threat from gamekeeper Biddle was stark and uncompromising, revealing a determination that the survey should not proceed and start a process that was bound to disrupt the peace and quiet of Stapleford Park and alter a whole way of life for a community totally unused to change.

Frow had been in the process of taking forward his end of the survey chain when a party of Stapleford estate tenants appeared, intent on blocking the passage of his crew. The survey intruders were ordered off the estate, but when they took no notice Biddle physically blocked their forward progress. Exasperated by this obstruction, Frow rushed at the determined gamekeeper and attempted to push him aside, but 'not succeeding in that, he immediately drew a pistol and threatened to shoot him.'

As the report in *The Builder* continues, 'a slight scuffle at once ensued; but, happily, the pistol was not discharged.' Even more

Protagonists:
Workers on the
North Midland Railway
Location:
The Rotherham area
Date:
1838-1840

fortunately, the arrival of a Midland Railway director, Lord Clinton, and one of the railway's London solicitors helped to defuse the situation. However, despite Mr Grindley, the solicitor, reading a letter purporting to be Lord Harborough's permission to survey, the latter's tenants and retainers would have none of it, and maintained their stand, giving the railway party no option but to retire.

The upshot of this little affair was an application from Biddle for a magistrate's warrant against Frow and the arrest of the latter at Melton Mowbray later in the day. The latter's rash behaviour cost him a weekend in prison and an appearance before the magistrate, the Rev G. E. Gillett, on the following Monday. The case was referred to the Assizes and Frow was granted bail on a personal surety of £100.

This incident was just one small part of a long and violent feud dealt with more fully in the next chapter, but it is not untypical of some of the extremes to which opposition to the early railways would go. There is no record of opposition to George Overton's survey for the route of the pioneer Stockton & Darlington Railway in 1818, but the surveyors of the Liverpool & Manchester scheme were not so fortunate. Whereas the S&D route lay in an area long accustomed to waggonways, the line of the Liverpool & Manchester Railway passed through virgin territory and its intrusion was seen with appropriate suspicion, especially by the big landowners.

The initial surveys for the L&M line were made by William James. The first of these, made in the summer of 1821, involved little more than preliminary sketches derived from riding over the countryside, but a second survey, commissioned at a fee of £300 and undertaken in 1822, involved a crew of six, one of whom was Robert Stephenson. Newly arrived from the cloistered halls of Edinburgh College, the latter must have been shocked at the antagonism the survey encountered.

The route surveyed by the James team skirted the southern edge of Chat Moss bog, then passed to the south of St Helens on a similar alignment to that eventually adopted. It was on this section that the surveyors ran foul of a mining community that feared that the railway would consume areas of coal reserves and thus imperil its livelihood. Stones were thrown and the surveyors threatened with being thrown down a coal shaft. So violent was the abuse directed at the man carrying the theodolite that James hired a prize-fighter for this task, and he soon had to justify his engagement in a gruelling fight with a collier. The prize-fighter did win, but the surveyor's party was nevertheless forced to retire under a barrage of stones, leaving behind the offending theodolite, then smashed to pieces.

As the years passed and the railway activity increased there were more and more reports of opposition to survey work. *The Builder* refers to a serious disturbance at Bicester when Farmer Dodwell confronted surveyors of the Bicester and Oxford line. There was another clash at nearby Islip, this time between surveyors and villagers, and railway surveyors were fined for trespass at Brentford and Macclesfield and for committing damage on the Duke of Buckingham's property at Westcott. The latter had also halted a survey at Haddesden, while other incidents were reported at South Tedworth, Osberton, Appleton and Glenfalloch. In his book *The Railway Surveyors* Gordon Biddle describes the near-clan warfare that accompanied the latter.

Of course there were many instances of co-operation between railways and landowners, but the former represented a new era and, like all things new, were feared and resented by some. The position was made no easier by the constraints placed upon the early railway schemes, which had many obstacles to overcome in the course of gestation. This process began with the formation of a group of interested parties, a round of meetings, soundings and other canvassing, then the issue of a prospectus and a start to the raising of capital. The financial response had to be sufficient to pay for the surveys and for legal and parliamentary expenses, as well as providing enough for a deposit on the proposed capital of the enterprise. To obtain the approval of Parliament, a Private Bill had first to be drafted and approved by the company's subscribers and Parliamentary Agents. To go with it a Petition seeking leave to introduce the Bill was required, and its deposit had to be accompanied by plans, sections, a book of reference and statements of costs, capital, subscriptions and officials, all lodged before 30 November of the current year. Earlier, notices had to be published in the London and Edinburgh Gazettes and in local newspapers, and interested parties advised of the promoters' intentions.

If the railway surveyors survived the opposition in the field, the promoters then had to face the problems of progressing their Bill through Parliament. After going before the Examiner of Petitions for Private Bills to be checked for compliance with Standing Orders, it was laid on the table of the House (circulated, in fact), then progressed to the Second Reading before reference back to a Committee of the House for detailed consideration. This was where the next major hurdles were encountered, usually in the form of opposition from rival schemes or other interested parties. Given the endorsement of the Committee and approval of the House at the Third Reading, the Bill still had to survive a similar process in the Lords.

The Great Western Railway scheme exemplifies the tribulations of the Parliamentary progress. At the Second Reading of the first Bill on 10 March 1834 the promoters ran headlong into fierce opposition to the Windsor branch from the Eton College authorities, who feared for the effect of the new railway upon their lads' attendance and morals. The Committee proceedings were to last for 57 days and, even though the Windsor branch proposal was dropped, the scheme failed to pass the subsequent Lords scrutiny and was rejected on 25 July.

In the following year the second Bill passed the Second Commons Committee reading on 9 March 1835, then survived a vicious attack on the potential safety of Box Tunnel to reach the Lords on 27 May 1835. By mid-June the Bill was before the Wharncliff Committee of the Lords, where it had another 40 days of contest, again with Box Tunnel featuring prominently in the questioning and evidence, before finally receiving the Royal Assent on 31 August 1835.

Getting the Royal Assent meant a great deal to any railway scheme, but in truth it was just a prelude to another period of difficulty in which land acquisition frequently proved slow and costly. Macdermot and Clinker refer to one example where a landowner built a 'house' of timber and brown paper on a piece of land needed for the railway in an attempt to inflate its asking price. Eventually, however, negotiation triumphed and it was possible to let the construction contracts and indulge in a little self-congratulation with a ceremony to mark the cutting of the first sod. But soon shareholders would be showing a marked reluctance to meet their 'calls' for capital, while the weather, the terrain and contractor inexperience or ineptitude regularly combined to push construction costs to unexpected heights. The workforce, too, contributed its share of aggravation, and while the story of these tough and hardy men has been

admirably told in volumes by Terry Coleman and David Brooke, it is worth including one example here before moving on to the inter-company conflicts.

The North Midland Railway was incorporated in 1836 with powers to build a line from Derby to Leeds. Opening of the southern section to Rotherham was on 11 May 1840, with completion through to Hunslet Lane, Leeds, on 1 July of that year. Along with many other railways in the Midlands and North, the North Midland contractors used Irish workers to augment its English labour contingents in the interests of getting on with the work quickly and thus hastening the day when traffic receipts would start to service the huge capital outlay. This scheme in particular was to encounter considerable antagonism between the two national factions, and to see it erupt into violent confrontation on more than one occasion.

On the NM line north of Rotherham Irish workers were being used on the section between Swinton and Darfield, and on 10 October 1838 a major row occurred with the neighbouring English gangs. It was reported in the *Doncaster Gazette* and the *Yorkshire Gazette* as follows:

'Between eleven and twelve o'clock on the forenoon of Wednesday last, the peaceable inhabitants of Rotherham were suddenly alarmed by a report that a serious disturbance had taken place between two parties of men who were working on the North Midland Railway, and that a large party were assembled on Masboro' Common, preparing for a desperate attack upon the town. In the course of a few minutes every shop in the High-street was closed. . .not a single shop was left without the shutters being put up and the door as securely fastened. . .

The following, as far as we can learn, are the facts of the case: On the line of the railway in the neighbourhood from Darfield to Swinton a number of Irishmen are employed against whom a jealousy had arisen on the part of the Englishmen, on account of the former

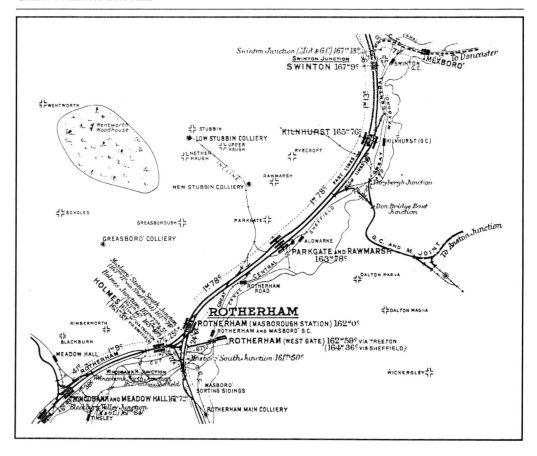

Rotherham and Swinton area lines, from Midland Railway Distance Diagrams.

working for a less rate of wages. On Wednesday morning, a dispute having arisen between one of each party, the Englishmen made common cause with their countryman, and suddenly commenced an attack in a body at Darfield by driving every Irishman away whom they found at work on the line. This they did from that place to Swinton, at the same time pulling down and destroying the mud hovels which the poor fellows had erected for the temporary residence of themselves and their families. This course was proceeded in until they came near Rotherham; when, the Irish beginning to gather courage as their forces increased, made their way over a number of fields, and broke down

all the fences, with the materials of which they armed themselves in the best way they could, several of them being already possessed of spades and other weapons. They then made a show of resistance, and stood their ground, determined not to be driven away any further.

Fortunately, at this time, Mr Stephenson, the contractor, with some of the directors, who happened that morning to be engaged in making a survey of some parts of the line, came between the parties. Mr Stephenson placed himself before the Irishmen, and promised to protect them if they would put themselves under his care, and otherwise there is little doubt but a great number of lives would have been lost. The poor fellows at once agreed to follow him, and Mr Stephenson led them peaceably into Rotherham, where he placed them in the yard of the Rotherham and Sheffield Railway in West-gate. Here he supplied them with a quantity of ale, and exhorted them to be peaceable, and they should be protected. Here the men, to the number of nearly 300, remained, apparently peaceably disposed, but loudly complaining of the injury which had been done by their enemies, and stating that two or three of their party had been killed already, and that they were obliged to act in self-defence.'

At this point the Irish group was visited by two local magistrates, Henry Walker of Clifton and Thomas Walker of Ravenfield. After pointing out the risks and consequences of riot, they went on to the English workers who were standing in groups around the North Midland route, some 600 in total, all of whom 'manifested a very bad spirit'. The magistrates put over the same message before returning to Rotherham where they felt sufficiently confident to dismiss the local troop of mounted yeomanry and to manage without the 40 artillerymen who arrived at 4 o'clock with their field piece. However, two parties of police, including special constables sworn in during the day, were kept on to patrol the streets of Rotherham and the Wath area throughout the night.

The day ended fairly calmly apart from 'the drunken brawls of some straggling parties of railway men'. Even so, the matter was not yet ended for, to quote the *Yorkshire Gazette* further:

'On Thursday, the disturbance again broke out more fearfully. The Englishmen appeared determined not to allow the Irish to work. A large number of the former congregated this afternoon in front of the residence of Mr Stephenson, and manifested a determination to pull down the house. In consequence of this display of feeling, and for the purpose of maintaining the public tranquillity, a detachment of artillery has arrived from Sheffield, and with the assistance of the special constables, have succeeded in apprehending a number of ringleaders. The riot act was then read by Henry Walker, Esq, of Clifton. The shops were all closed, and there was a total suspension of business.'

Eventually the Rotherham conflict fizzled out, but the North Midland was to experience more trouble in June 1839 when the luckless Irish were chased across the fields around Oakenshaw Viaduct. Yet another conflict then followed in 1840 at Glass Houghton. In the course of the latter, after the North Midland navvies at Methley had run out of money and drink on Easter Monday, they took it into their heads on the Tuesday to attack a party of Stephenson's Irish contingent on the nearby works of the York & North Midland. There they 'broke into their cottages, assaulted their wives, stole their possessions and proceeded to such an extent to their lawless and daring outrages that it was found necessary to send express to Leeds for a police force'.

Meantime violent fighting had broken out, and Stephenson's efforts to warn the attackers of the folly of their actions only produced a volley of stones that felled him. In the end a squad of armed Metropolitan policemen, part of a general move to employ these skilled troubleshooters in areas of potential violence, managed to bring the conflict under control and capture the ringleaders.

The navvies were involved in other serious affrays, notably in Scotland and on the Lancaster & Carlisle Railway, but on the whole they were a surprisingly skilled, hard-working and well-behaved community.

2
DRAMA IN STAPLEFORD PARK

In 1844 Stapleford Park, a pleasant private estate located some four miles east of Melton Mowbray, was the home of Lord and Lady Harborough. Lying in a pastoral, wooded area of Leicestershire, a feature of the park was the River Eye that wound its way through the grounds. A second waterway, the Oakham Canal, was routed round the east side of the area.

The previous earl had supported the canal scheme when it was originally mooted in 1792, and had later left it money in his will. The canal route had been agreed with the earl and the waterway harmonised with the estate, which also used it for the carriage of inwards coal and outwards produce. From its opening in 1800-03 the canal had brought useful benefits to the whole area, although it could hardly be considered a runaway financial success due to the periods of water shortage that hindered or halted operations. There were, of course, some differences between estate and canal, but on the whole, they lived in reasonable harmony and the waterway was an accepted part of a tranquil rural scene where agriculture and husbandry were the main activities.

There had been railway proposals for the area ever since the London Northern Rail Road scheme of 1825, one of them suggesting a line from the Oakham Canal on to Stamford. But nothing came of any of these. The 1836 Norwich & Leicester and South Midland Counties projects were followed by the 1840 London & Great Northern Trunk Railway, then by the Lynn & Leicester

Protagonists:
Lord Harborough and the
Midland Railway

Location:
Stapleford Park, Leics

Date:
13-16 November 1844
and subsequently

Railway. A contemporary scheme from the Midland Railway, that of the Syston & Peterborough, was then approved at a special general meeting of the company on 8 October 1844, after which the rival Lynn & Leicester faded from the scene.

Once the MR decision had been taken, the pressure was on to complete the preparatory work by 30 November in order to lodge a Bill with Parliament within the statutory time limit. A series of public meetings was held, a diversion agreed to appease the inhabitants of the Uppingham area and preliminary approaches made to influential people, including Lord Harborough and the canal proprietors. The former was unimpressed and made it clear that the railway could expect no co-operation from himself or his tenants.

One side of the case argued for the railway because the existing turnpike was 'a very hilly, expensive road', but at a meeting at Oakham on 23 October and attended by George

The Syston-Peterborough line at Melton Mowbray in Midland Railway days. *Lens of Sutton*

The Saxby area from Midland Railway Distance Diagrams, showing Stapleford Park south of the junction.

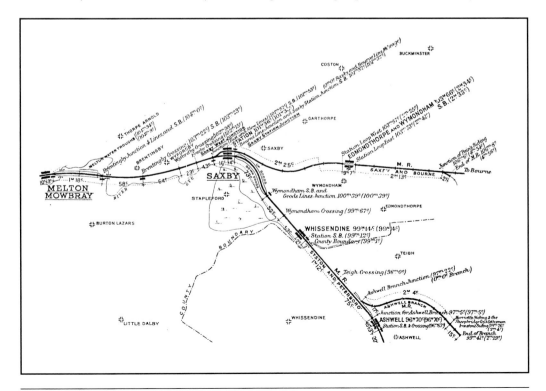

Hudson, George Stephenson and John Ellis, one William Latham was vociferous in his opposition, haranguing his audience with a long and lively address on behalf of Lord Harborough, the canal and carrier interests, and his own. He maintained that the Midland was only interested in the line as a counter to the proposals of the London & York Railway, and that Lord Harborough would go and live in Switzerland if the intrusion ever came about. Latham waxed lyrical over the plight of the road interests, declaring:

'I shall also oppose it [the railway scheme] on behalf of Mr Guydo Dickenson, the carrier from Melton to Leicester. Mr Dickenson, who has a wife and eight children, has expended a considerable sum in erecting warehouses and purchasing wagons to carry on his occupation, never dreaming of so wild a project. If it succeeds Mr Dickenson, like many others, will be a ruined man and he will have to journey to a court which I am constrained occasionally to call the Infernal Court of Bankruptcy of Birmingham.'

A full record of the Latham outpouring appeared in *Payne's Leicester & Midland Counties Advertiser* of 2 November 1844, but it failed to prevent the meeting passing four

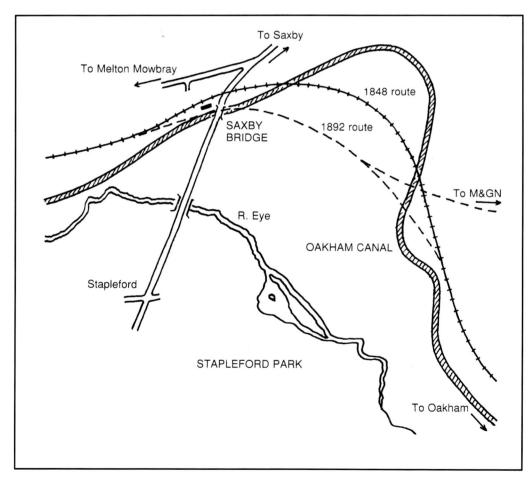

The Syston & Peterborough Railway and Oakham Canal at Saxby Bridge.

resolutions in favour of the Syston & Peterborough scheme.

Despite the remaining opposition to its plans the Midland Railway could not tolerate any delay in its preparatory work if the Parliamentary deadline was to be met. Accordingly it pushed ahead with surveying, the survey team reaching the Stapleford Park area in the middle of November and, despite Lord Harborough's known position, entering the park proper on Wednesday 13 November. A party of seven 'railway levellers' or 'railwayers', as the *Leicestershire Chronicle* called them, tried to approach the forbidden area by the canal towpath, believing that they would be free from interference on such a public right of way. They were wrong. A party of nine of Lord Harborough's men intercepted them before surveying work could start and took them prisoner. Unceremoniously the hapless captives were hauled off by cart, along with the tools of their unwanted profession, to Cold Overton Hall, the home of the nearest magistrate.

It was later claimed that as they neared Cold Overton one of the estate men arrived with the suggestion that the captives be shot, but no doubt that was only play-acting and their captors contented themselves with merely tipping the prisoners out of the cart. The magistrate was away from home, so two of the captives were permitted to go to Oakham to obtain professional assistance. Mr Hough, the Syston & Peterborough secretary, duly arrived in a chaise, but magistrate Turner had still not returned, creating something of a dilemma for both captives and captors alike. Eventually, having spent most of the day on the exercise, both parties decided to separate for the night and return to the fray on the following day, but the estate party did hang on to the railway theodolite as a token of their victory.

And return to the fray they did, as the *Advertiser*'s issue of 16 November recorded:

'Lord Harborough and the Midland Railway Co.
Another skirmish took place on Thursday morning last, between Lord Harborough's retainers, and the survey-

ors and solicitors in the employ of the Midland Railway Company. The scene of the action was Saxelby Bridge, adjoining His Lordship's park. After the defeat of the surveyors on the previous day, it was generally understood that another attempt on a larger scale was to be made on the following morning. Consequently by nine o'clock between thirty and forty of His Lordship's servants assembled at the spot above named, to prevent the surveyors of the company making levels on the towing path of the Oakham Canal, and along Stapleford Park. Very soon posses of gentlemen in the employ of the company arrived in chaises etc from Melton and Oakham, heading a number of reckless-looking "ragamuffins", carrying flags high and staffs etc and looking in the distance very much like a regiment of soldiers coming to take the place by storm.

A lengthy parley took place on the bridge between His Lordship's steward and solicitor, the clerk and treasurer of the Oakham Canal Company and the solicitors and surveyors of the railway company, as to the mode of proceeding to be adopted. Meantime, Lord Harborough's men made preparations for a determined stand on the towing path and each side of the bridge by fencing the path across with drays etc close to the water's edge. An attempt was made by the surveyors to force their way through the party stationed on the open side of the bridge but the barrier was too firm to be broken, and they had to beat a retreat. After this a delay took place during which other bodies of men from Oakham and Stamford were added to the railway ranks, and fresh reinforcements joined His Lordship's standard.

Four or five county police now came up and stated it to be their intention, if possible, to prevent a breach of the peace; and that they should arrest the first person who committed an assault. But the parties then decided to lay aside their weapons, consisting of stout shillelaghs etc and were ordered not to strike any blows, but simply to try to offset strength by pushing. A great stand was then made by His Lordship's party below the bridge, nearest Melton, who stood wedged together and forming a living and very formidable-looking barrier. The surveyors next placed rows of their men with their backs to the faces of the earl's team and set others in an opposite position to force the way.

An almost indescribable scene now took place. The Railwayists exerted their utmost strength; but so firmly did His Lordship's party retain their ground that more than one person was forced up high in the air, between and rolling over the heads of the contending party. Others were kneeling in the ditch, amid the shouts of the leaders and the laughter of numerous spectators. Great confusion now ensued, the two armies mixing together, and in the tumult and dirt becoming almost indistinguishable. Amid this confusion the surveyors succeeded in getting the chain they were bearing on forbidden ground. Lord

Harborough's men then took forcible possession of the chain which, in the scuffle to recover it, was broken in two places.

A fine chase was then had for about a quarter of a mile down the towpath - affording the numerous spectators on the bridge almost as humorous and exciting a pleasure as a "run after reynard". Another barrier was then about to be formed when a truce was shouted by the railwayists. Then it was finally agreed that each party should withdraw their forces, that the matter should be judiciously brought before the magistrates by issuing a summons for assault against one or two of the men from each party, which it is understood will be heard at the Petty Sessions at Melton Mowbray on Tuesday next.'

The newspaper report concludes with confirmation that the Clerk and Treasurer of the Oakham Canal Company, the notable William Latham, was on the scene; indeed, he may even have been the reporter! He was certainly the chief negotiator on the opposi-

The view from Saxby Bridge with the line of bushes marking the former route of the Oakham Canal, and the trackbed of the original railway in the background.

tion side and firmly believed that his discussion with Mr Morris, who was railway clerk to the Midland's solicitors Berridge & Macaulay, and with Mr Hough, meant both parties giving up the right to action until the matter had been brought before the courts. The newspaper comments also revealed that the canal company had earlier given up to Lord Harborough its rights in the towing path, but a court decision subsequently held this to be improper.

A separate report on this incident says that after the police warning, 'each party, reluctant to draw upon it another enemy, wisely resolved to eschew striking.' It also draws a graphic picture of the railway tactics of using its front rank as wedges to be rammed into the enemy by the charge of the rear rank, a truly novel tactic.

Although the pushing war had ended, any Stapleford gloating that the railway activity had been seriously delayed was to prove premature. The following day, a Friday, passed quietly enough, but by the evening rumours were beginning to circulate to the effect that the railway party had no intention of remaining inactive until the Tuesday and was already gathering further reinforcements. The news came from the public houses in Oakham and neighbouring villages, which found themselves inundated with strangers seeking accommodation for the night. They came from Stamford, Peterborough and more distant parts of the Midland Railway and carried an air of purpose that did not go unnoticed.

Fabling, Lord Harborough's steward, was not slow to react to this new threat. He called a council of war on the Friday evening and in the dark, bleak early hours of Saturday morning the defenders were again gathered together and set about the task of building more barricades. They used wagons and hurdles to build a line of formidable defences, and even brought in the estate fire engine ready to discourage attackers with a hosing down. The engine was placed at the point where previous attacks had taken place, but Fabling had no means of knowing where the next blow would fall and was compelled to spread his men thinly over the various weak

points of the 800-acre park.

The restless Latham set out to reconnoitre on horseback with a few cronies, but as luck would have it he chose to ride via Whissendine and Langham. As he did so the enemy, armed with staves, flagstaffs and billhooks, was marching via Ashwell and Teigh. By the time Latham got to Oakham they had gone, but this did not prevent him putting pen to paper and serving a warning upon one of Berridge & Macaulay's clerks who was still in his bedroom:

'To Messrs Berridge & Macaulay, their clerk or agents, and Mr Hough

Dear Sirs,
I was very sorry to receive information early this morning of your intentions of again attempting by force to go along the towing path and Lord Harborough and Mr Fabling's land contrary to the promises made by you and your agents on Thursday last. You then agreed that all hostilities should cease until we had been before the magistrates. I beg to give you notice, though I much dislike physical force, that we are fully prepared for you. We have barricaded the towing path and have in readiness a few cannon from Lord Harborough's yacht. If you force us to use them, as a last resort, the blood be upon your heads.
I am, dear sirs, yours faithfully,
William Latham'

From the barricades messages were sent to the magistrates and police warning them of the likely affray, but some were away from home and for others the notice was just too early. Mr Macaulay, who was also clerk to the Leicestershire magistrates, was seen to head through Melton towards Saxby, but no one quite knew where his sympathies would lie.

About 7 o'clock, as dawn was finally breaking, a party of about ten railwaymen had appeared on the towing path at the Melton end of the estate and tried to break through the barricades there. They made no impression, but, as this small conflict was get-

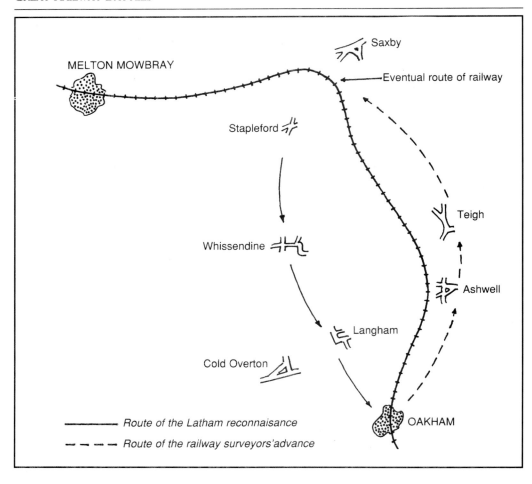

Battle of Saxby 'troop movements' on 16 November 1844.

ting into its stride, something like a hundred men, led by railway law clerk Morris and surveyors Cope, Rosper and Colthurst, had swarmed over the park railings on the Oakham side and, overwhelming the small opposition there, had quickly put to work four chain gangs in an effort to carry out their tasks quickly and while the defenders were otherwise occupied. Their route took them towards Lord Harborough's cottage, and this proved too much for the gallant Fabling who gathered a few men round him and galloped over to the scene of action, determined to stem the breakthrough. Cope warned the steward that if he was not to risk being hurt he had better retire and, when Fabling declined, ordered his men to remove him.

'Go for the chains,' was Fabling's reaction and matched his own actions to those words. With him was Brown, the local lock-keeper of the canal, and a man of great size and strength. At every blow he sent a man flying and soon the whole affair was even more violent than the previous encounters, with the railway party 'thrusting their spikes into the sides of the defendants of the park' and the latter wrenching the weapons from them and defending themselves as best they could. The noise could be heard in villages for miles around, and aroused more of the workers and tenantry who, holding the steward in consid-

The former Crown Hotel at Oakham, where the MR officials lodged in 1844,
is now a shopping and residential complex.

erable respect, soon added their weight to his struggle. Slowly the estate staff gained the upper hand, and by the time Lord Harborough appeared, aroused from his sickbed by the affray, the railwayists were ready to run. As the newspaper records, 'after many broken heads, wounded faces and sides, the lower grade of the intruders gave way.'

Gradually the tumult subsided leaving the railway party standing with heads down and their weapons broken and discarded. Some bore the scars of the conflict, and many of His Lordship's defenders had cuts and bruises described as painful but not dangerous. The victorious Fabling, in no mood to leave the matter inconclusive, declared that the railway ringleaders could not leave the park until he had details of their names and addresses. Ten were held back for this process and the lesser fry allowed to depart.

Cope, of 29 Temple Row, Birmingham, and Colthurst, of 40 Gracechurch Street, London, were among the professional men whose details were recorded. Others were labourers, perhaps railway gangers or part of the hired prize-fighter contingent, and came from Nottingham, Derby, Birmingham and more local places. After some sorting out back at the respective headquarters a crop of cases came before the courts, the Midland Railway seeking warrants against Lord Harborough, Mr Fabling and Mr Latham and summoning Mr Todd of the estate staff for assault. These efforts failed, but the case against the railway ringleaders was referred to a superior court, with various others being bound over.

The railway six appeared at Leicester Spring Assizes on Tuesday 25 March 1845 before Lord Chief Justice Tyndal. Witnesses then shed further light on the bitter battles of the previous November, Fabling admitting that he had recruited defenders at 2s 6d per day and the Midland contending that its surveyors had just done their duty. However, they were clearly organised as a coherent force, with white tape in their buttonholes or hats, and several witnesses gave evidence of aggressive tactics. One maintained that a man with a staff had placed it between his legs and rolled him down after shouting 'If you value your life, go back or I will chop you down'. Another defender alleged himself attacked by a man with a staff with brass nails in it, who threatened to 'job it down his throat' if he did not retire.

Witness William Grooby stated that Colthurst had stabbed at him twice and pierced his coat. He maintained that Tupper had suffered a similar attack, but had been fortunate in having the point turned by the contents of his pocket and suffering only a bruised arm. Eventually the court found the

defendants guilty of an assault upon Grooby and sentenced them to one month's first class imprisonment with a fine of 1 shilling on release. A Nisi Prius court on the same day awarded one of the railway surveyors £8 for the loss of his theodolite.

As the dust settled on these events the Midland made an agreement to purchase the Oakham Canal for £26,000 plus a share allocation. This was announced during the passage of the Syston & Peterborough Bill through the House and helped to secure its approval, contained in an Act of 30 June 1845. The Act protected Lord Harborough's position with a period of 12 months for negotiation, and to counter this the Midland started to survey alternative routes in the

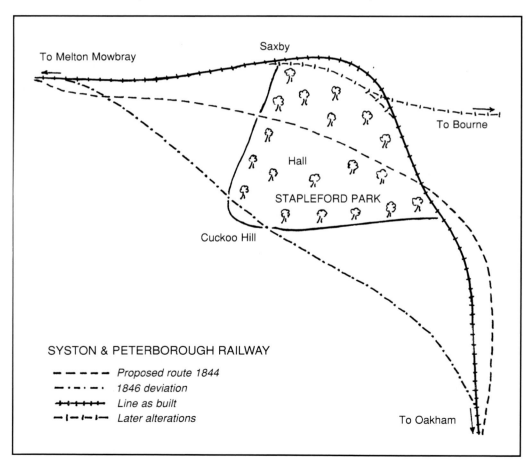

SYSTON & PETERBOROUGH RAILWAY

- – – – – Proposed route 1844
- – · – · – 1846 deviation
+++++ Line as built
– I – I – I – Later alterations

Routes of the Syston & Peterborough Railway.

Stapleford Park area, a process that again brought the conflict of interests out into the open. There were more confrontations and survey obstruction, only solved by carrying out the work with the surveyors travelling on the roof of a carriage!

By the middle of 1846 it began, at last, to look as if the railway project might be getting somewhere. On 18 June an Act was passed authorising deviations to the original route through Stapleford Park, one passing to the south-west via Cuckoo Hill plantation and the other alternative north-east along the course of the canal. On 1 September, the date on which the railway from Syston to Melton was opened, the contract for the Melton-Oakham section was let to Thomas Dyson who got to work straight away. In between these two events the Midland had brought another case against Lord Harborough, 100 of whose staff

were tried at Nottingham but found not guilty.

The Deviation Act had stipulated that the line should be carried through Cuckoo Hill without surface disturbance, a condition that proved impossible to observe. The work of tunnelling through the hill resulted in the destruction of a number of trees and further complaint from Lord Harborough. At last, however, the MR was able to resolve the long-standing dispute by paying over the sum of £25,000 to his lordship and agreeing to use the canal route which lay further from Stapleford Hall. The company did save £35,000 in its construction costs by this action, but saddled itself with a need for severe speed restrictions on what became known as 'Lord Harborough's Curve'. This was not eased until 1892, when the first Saxby station was closed after 44 years and replaced by a new one on a fresh deviation of easier curvature.

Opened in 1892 and closed in 1961, the second station at Saxby was in a sad state of dereliction when pictured here in 1993.

3
THE GOING GETS TOUGH

The emergence of the Stockton & Darlington Railway scheme, now honoured for its pioneering achievements, was by no means a consensus affair. A strong body of those interested in providing an outlet for West Durham coal would have preferred a line passing well north of Darlington, and although the interests of that town and neighbouring Yarm eventually triumphed, the supporters of the northern scheme were by no means satisfied to leave matters as they were. Instead, they set about forming a breakaway group, which, in turn, was responsible for the setting up of the Tees & Weardale Railway project that planned an alternative line to the north bank of the River Tees, near Haverton Hill. Some measure of the justification for this group lies in the fact that the Stockton & Darlington itself soon needed to consider extension to deeper water downstream, but rejected Haverton Hill as its new port in favour of Middlesbrough. Bills for a Tees & Weardale Railway were strongly opposed by the Stockton & Darlington party and, largely as a result, were rejected by Parliament in 1824 and 1825.

The Stockton & Darlington line was opened throughout on 27 September 1825 and quickly justified the faith of its promoters. Its very success brought the need to reach deeper water and larger vessels, resulting in authorisation of the extension to Middlesbrough on 23 May 1828. On the same day the Tees & Weardale party, now honouring the Duke of Clarence by using his name, secured its Clarence Railway Act for a

| **Protagonists:** |
| Clarence Railway versus Stockton & Darlington and Great North of England, Clarence & Hartlepool Junction railways |
| **Location:** |
| Near Ferryhill, Co Durham |
| **Date:** |
| 1839-45 |

line from Haverton Hill westward to a junction with the S&D main line at Sim Pasture Farm. This would provide a route for coal

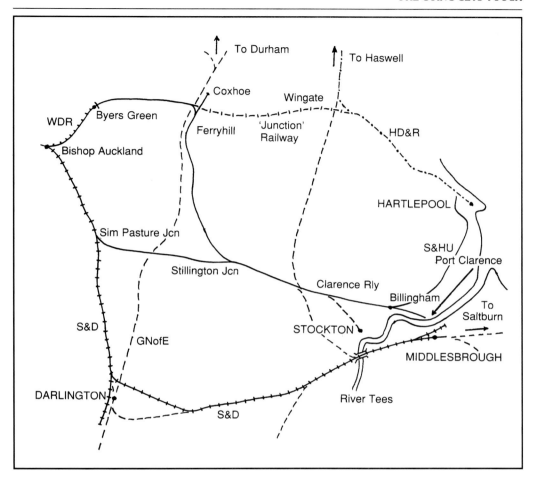

The Clarence Railway and neighbouring lines.

from West Durham to a deep-water stretch of the Tees 5 miles shorter than that of the Stockton & Darlington, and the proprietors of the latter were under no illusions as to the effect of this development upon their business.

In addition to approving the main line, the Clarence Act authorised three branches, one of which was to the Deanery at St Andrews Auckland. This would have given the Clarence Railway direct access to a coal-producing area to supplement the business handed over from the S&D route, but the company was unable to secure the consent of the Earl of Eldon to traffic passing over his land and thus found itself in something of a

cleft stick, having authority for a shorter line than that of its rival but being dependent on the latter for the supply of traffic. As the S&D also controlled the tolls for the carriage as far as Sim Pasture, it enjoyed quite a strong position in the matter.

As part of its strategy for getting out of this dependent situation, the Clarence Railway sought another access route to the coalfields, dropping two of its authorised branches in favour of a route north from its main line at Stillington to Elvet Street, Durham. This was authorised by an Act of 1 June 1829 along with branches continuing further north to Sherburn via Coxhoe and west to Byers Green, the latter designed to

The London end of Newton Aycliffe station on a wet day in 1993.
Sim Pasture Junction lay straight ahead, near the footbridge.

provide an alternative access route to the West Durham coal deposits. Armed with this muscle, Henry Blanshard, for the Clarence party, tried to conclude a deal with the S&D for building a link from Sim Pasture to Elstrob on the proposed City of Durham branch. This would have given the Stockton & Darlington a share in the shorter route, but that body had fought so hard for its railway that it was in no mood to surrender anything, certainly not to mere possibilities, which was all that the Clarence plans represented at this stage.

Relations between the pioneer S&D and its Clarence imitator became increasingly based on mutual suspicion, and Joseph Pease of the Stockton & Darlington was later to accuse the Clarence of making 'a sinister attempt to obtain the sanction of the Legislature to a branch railway calculated to injure their line by depriving it of traffic.' Not to be outdone, Christopher Tennant, on behalf of the Clarence interests, suggested that the S&D was 'trying to get possession of the county'.

By the middle of 1833 construction work on the Clarence Railway's original line was sufficiently advanced for coal to start moving to Stockton, and by the following January it was being shipped through new staiths at Haverton Hill, the shipment area now being called Port Clarence. In that year the Clarence was to earn £2,206 6s 2d, but the S&D charge of $2\frac{1}{4}$d per ton mile on coal handed over to the newcomer at Sim Pasture was seriously restricting traffic, and the earnings figure was well below the cost of running the new railway.

The CR had reached the Ferryhill area from Stillington on its main line on 16 January 1834, but its capital was exhausted and there were no funds left to build the Byers Green branch and secure its own access to the West Durham coal traffic. In addition to the funding problems, the Durham ecclesiastical interests were expressing their opposition to the railway's plans in the shape of extravagant land compensation claims. The first years of the Clarence Railway were certainly proving tough.

An early engraving of coal-loading activity in the North East.

Clarence revenue rose to £3,348 in 1835, a year which also saw the Stillington-Coxhoe line carrying a passenger service, with an omnibus link to Durham City. By 1836 Clarence earnings were up to £6,778, but the company was still a long way from making a profit. In desperation the Byers Green project was revived and the West Durham Railway approached for funds. With the help of a party of its own Clarence shareholders, work got under way in October 1836 and a rather inadequate, poor-standard temporary line was brought into use on 31 March 1837. Enough had been done to obtain a Parliamentary certificate, and on the strength of this modest success the Clarence Railway issued a new prospectus for the capital required to complete the branch to a proper standard.

Unfortunately for the Clarence, fate was already conspiring against it in another direction. The Hartlepool Docks & Railway enterprise had obtained an Act on 1 June 1832 covering the construction of a new dock and a railway to feed it with shipment coal. The latter was opened as far as Haswell on 23 November 1835. Although the dock company could not manage to complete the remainder of the lines authorised to it, part of this mantle was assumed by the Great North

of England, Clarence & Hartlepool Junction Railway, a short line designed to link the companies detailed in its long title by running 8½ miles westwards from Wingate on the dock company's line to a point just north of Ferryhill, where there would be links north and south to the (eventual) main line and a direct connection to the Byers Green branch. The 'Junction' railway, as it came to be known, secured its Act on 3 July 1837 and began construction immediately. Here was the promise of more trouble for the struggling Clarence Railway, for traffic from West Durham over the Byers Green branch would hardly travel the '21 miles 1 furlong 3 links' to Port Clarence via Stillington when it could take the shorter route over the Junction line to that of the HD&R, and also enjoy privileged dock charges on arrival at Hartlepool.

As construction of the Junction company's line from Wingate to Ferryhill progressed, the Clarence directors were thinking up a counter-manoeuvre. A group of them promoted the Stockton & Hartlepool Union Railway, an 8-mile link between the Clarence main line at Billingham and Hartlepool, where the new company planned to build its own dock. The rail route would be much longer than rival routes, but tolls could be reduced to offset this and coal-shippers offered a combined rail and dock package. Under this threat the HD&R agreed with the S&HU on a single dock and equal rates, while the Clarence also agreed to provide the West Durham coal-owners with a free choice of route in return for a guarantee of 15,000 tons of traffic annually.

With remarkably rapid speed the West Durham Railway, which had been authorised by an Act of 4 July 1837, was carrying traffic in less than a year. The use of wayleaves rather than land purchase had helped, but initially only token loads were possible as the Clarence company's onward Byers Green branch was not properly completed. In fact, on 3 August 1841 a committee of the Clarence Railway was earnestly appealing for additional funds, for revenue was still not up to expectations and at least two collieries had recently diverted their traffic. A notice issued by the secretary, Charles Benson, from the Clarence Railway Office at 80 Old Broad Street, London, detailed a resolution passed at a Special General Meeting of the proprietors:

'That an urgent and earnest appeal be made to each individual Proprietor, strongly soliciting the subscription of £5 per Share on his respective interest, to carry through the remaining works, and defray the present claims on the Company; and that an early answer should be requested to the same.'

The notice continued:

'The whole of the works of the Railway, both on the main line and the branches, are now completed with the exception of a small part of the Byers Green branch, the expense of which will not exceed £1,000, and which will be finished in less than two months. Your Railroad then will be in a state to receive the large and rapidly increasing traffic from the numerous Pits which have been opened out around it.'

The permanent West Durham line was completed to Billy Row on 15 June 1841, and full through working over the Byers Green branch began four months later.

In addition to the various strategic ploys used by the Clarence Railway to break out of its difficulties and increase traffic levels, it was also involved in two curious tactical situations. At the western end of the Byers Green branch the West Durham line was virtually an extension and the two railways shared a common enemy in the Stockton & Darlington. Even so, this did not prevent the Clarence from applying the lesson it had learned from its dependence on the S&D at Sim Pasture and using a clever device to ensure that any coal passing from West Durham should be routed via Stillington Junction.

During the piecemeal construction of the line from Ferryhill to Byers Green, the Clarence Railway ended its stretch just under 100 yards short of West Durham land. When the powers in the original authorising Act ran out, this section was no longer subject to the maximum tolls laid down in the 1829 Act and the Clarence was able to lay permanent rails over it and complete the end-on junction, with the resultant section then being free from statutory charging control. Thus any traffic destined for Hartlepool over the Junction line could be actively discouraged by high tolls, and that via the longer Clarence route given favourable treatment. The section concerned was marked by obelisks at each end, and it was not until 1843 that the Junction company was able to get this weapon removed. By petitioning Parliament it then succeeded in having Clause 30 inserted in the 1843 Clarence Railway Act, which limited the tolls to be charged on the disputed section.

At the eastern end of the Byers Green branch the Clarence Railway proved equally difficult and was aided in that process by a significant piece of good fortune. The Junction railway's Act of 1837 had recorded detailed powers for bridging the Great North of England Railway, but had not been specific about crossing the Clarence's Coxhoe/Sherburn branch. No doubt the legislators

The railways at Cornforth, near
Ferryhill, Co Durham.

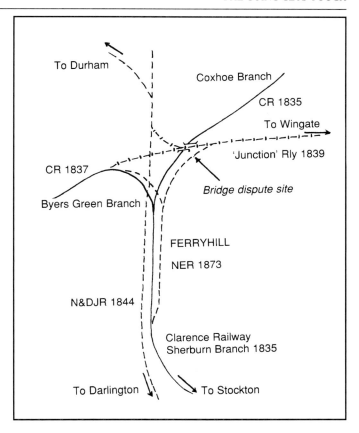

considered the power to connect with the
Byers Green branch was sufficient, but whatever the reason, no specific crossing or access
authority was given and the Clarence saw no
reason to provide such facilities for one of its
arch-enemies.

The line from Wingate had reached
Thrislington on 11 July 1839, and from there
the intention was that it should throw out
spurs north and south, with the Byers Green
branch connection continuing straight
ahead. One crossing was laid in and promptly
removed by Clarence employees, not without
some justification, for three level crossings of
its route within such a short distance would
have made it almost impossible to operate.
Recognising this, the Junction Railway
offered to locate the point of separation of
the three routes west of the Clarence's
Coxhoe/Sherburn branch, which would then
only be crossed once, but the Clarence was in

no mood to throw away its obstructional
advantage and would have none of the idea.

A war of attrition was now in full swing
with the Junction company trying to press
ahead on the strength of its original
Parliamentary approval and the Clarence
determined it should not succeed. The latter
obtained an injunction in August 1841 halting the Junction's construction work and
forcing that company to approach Parliament
again. In an Act of 28 July 1843 the Junction
company was given specific powers to bridge
the Coxhoe branch and the GNofE, now the
Newcastle & Darlington Junction. Much
good it did them, for when work recom-
menced in the December of 1843 a gang of
labourers appeared on the site and threatened the construction workers with physical
violence if they persisted in their labours.
There seems little doubt that the threateners
were prompted and paid by the Clarence

Railway or its agent, but an appeal to the magistrates was unable to establish this and proved inconclusive.

The next step by the exasperated Junction company was to build the bridge piers on its own land rather than try to gain access to that of the Clarence company, but the latter was not, by any means, ready to give in. It promptly built a couple of walls on its own property, but in such a position as to prevent the completion of the Junction's bridge. A pamphlet war was launched at the same time and it took another Act of Parliament before any more progress was made. Even then the Junction company needed a further injunction to prevent more interference with its works. It was to be November 1845 before the first mineral traffic was exchanged from the Byers Green branch to the Junction line *en route* to Hartlepool Dock. The Clarence had finally had to give way, but had been able to hold matters up for six years by its orchestrated policy of obstruction.

To some extent the Clarence rearguard action had worked. Some collieries that might

have routed traffic via the Sherburn branch did divert to the Junction line, but the beleaguered Clarence Railway was able to hold on to a significant and increasing volume of West Durham coal via Byers Green and the City of Durham branch. Revenue had risen from £19,000 in 1840 to £23,000 in 1841, but competition from the Junction and S&D routes meant that rates had to be kept low, and sufficient profit to reduce the company's loan debt was still near impossible. A meeting on 17 February 1842 was given the improving revenue figure and news of the completion of the Byers Green branch, but also had to hear that:

'Coals sent to market have not as yet proved so hard as could be wished. . . two Collieries have ceased from working for a few weeks, but your Committee see no reason to doubt the general quality of the large bed of unworked Coal opened out by this Branch.'

This meeting also heard, with some delight, that the S&D had been the loser in a private

The remains of the disputed bridge over the former Clarence Railway Coxhoe branch at West Cornforth in 1962. *Ken Hoole Study Centre*

action in the Court of Common Pleas against the level of its charges, and that the Vice Chancellor had confirmed the trespass injunction against the Junction Railway. It reported a decision to reject the S&D's proposals for a temporary passenger service to Durham via Sim Pasture, Stillington and Quarrington pending completion of the Great North of England line. The Clarence was clearly still at war.

By 5 October 1842 this intransigence and the inter-railway rivalry was proving costly. The Clarence shareholders were being told that the Exchequer Loan Commissioners had taken over the company and were planning to sell it to recover a debt of £155,000, although the lines had earned a surplus of £4,995 in 1840 and £7,940 in 1841, and a surplus of £12,100 was expected in 1842. By the time the debts to bondholders and other creditors were added, the total owing was over a quarter of a million pounds, making the outlook something less than rosy.

Fortunately the response to a further appeal for support was good, and a new committee of management was able to deal with the Loan Commissioners and recover their railway. New capital was raised and by 1845 improved working and traffic levels had lifted the earnings to £43,148 against expenses of £23,118. Of the revenue figure half was payable to the Stockton & Hartlepool Railway, which had taken over the working of the Clarence under a 21-year lease operable from 2 September 1844.

By an Act of 30 June 1852 the Stockton & Hartlepool amalgamated with the Hartlepool West Harbour & Dock Company and took over the Clarence Railway. The atmosphere of contention and dispute gave way to a greater realism and the fighting Clarence eventually passed to the North Eastern Railway in 1865. The old main line of the Clarence Railway did come into new prominence with the scheme of electrification completed on 1 July 1915 for the movement of West Durham coal from Shildon to Newport, but with typical Clarence luck traffic did not reach expected levels and the scheme lasted for only 20 years. In the same vein the Clarence Railway's Sherburn branch got only as far as Coxhoe and the link between the Byers Green and Wingate lines lasted only until the 1850s. The Byers Green branch proper closed on 2 May 1966.

On the main line north from Darlington it is still possible to spot the point at which the Clarence Railway's route crossed on its way to Sim Pasture Junction. There the course has been largely overlaid by an industrial estate served by Newton Aycliffe station, itself almost on the site of the actual junction. At Ferryhill short stubs of the Junction line and the Sherburn branch continued in use for freight after Ferryhill had lost its main-line station, but the disputed bridge itself no longer stands as a memorial to an early example of railway guerilla warfare.

4
A RAILWAY STATION
TAKEN BY STORM

The great city of Carlisle is noted, among other things, for its complex and colourful history. Its border location made it a strategic front-line stronghold in the long and bitter struggles between the English and Scots nations, when huge armies, punitive raiders and the local reivers all took their turns in marching back and forth, intent on any mischief from full-scale conflict to the acquisition of a neighbour's cattle. At one period it seemed as if the aspirations of rival railways might continue the tradition, and one incident in particular, at Crown Street station, had a lot in common with the earlier border raids.

The first railway to serve Carlisle was the pioneer Newcastle & Carlisle, built across the narrow neck of northern England partly for strategic reasons, partly for coal carriage and partly to shorten the passage for goods from the Continent to Ireland and the Cumbrian coast. The company was incorporated by an Act of 22 May 1829, but it was 1834 before the first traffic started to move, using horses as the motive power. Locomotive-hauled trains began between Blaydon and Hexham on 9 March 1835, with extension to Haydon Bridge on 28 June 1835 and a western end, from Blenkinsopp Colliery at Greenhead to a station in London Road, Carlisle, opening on 19 July. In the following year the N&CR opened a short branch to the inland end of the Carlisle Canal, and on 18 June 1838 it completed its route through to Gateshead to fulfil the promoters' original objectives.

Protagonists:
Lancaster & Carlisle Railway and
Maryport & Carlisle Railway

Location:
Crown Street station, Carlisle

Date:
Saturday 17 March 1849

While the Newcastle & Carlisle line was under construction, commercial and industrial interests in and around Maryport began lobbying support for a scheme that would extend rail communication to their own area. The promoters encountered a lot of enthusiasm and interest, and on 12 July 1837 secured an Act for the Maryport & Carlisle Railway, which was to be constructed from each end inwards using the £180,000 capital authorised by the Act.

The first section of the M&C, between Maryport and Arkleby, was opened on 15 July 1840, with a short extension to Aspatria following on 12 April of the following year. At the Carlisle end progress was slower, but a line from there to Wigton was eventually opened on 3 May 1843, with a coach link then operating over the uncompleted middle section. The M&C inaugural train actually ran through to the Newcastle & Carlisle company's London Road station, but the public service that began on 10 May used a station at Bogfield where the M&C line

The railways of Carlisle in 1849.

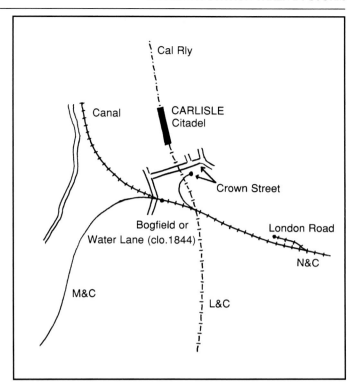

joined its ally's Canal branch. Spasmodic work on the uncompleted centre section culminated in the eventual opening of the whole route on 10 February 1845.

The M&C temporary station at Bogfield, variously referred to by that name or as Water Lane, was rather less than convenient. It had access to the city via Currock Road, but was well away from the main commercial and civic development. Accordingly, the M&C directors accompanied the arrival of the first train at Carlisle with the announcement that they were to provide the city with a new and more accessible station on a 7-acre site that had been specially purchased for the purpose off Crown Street. John Dobson, to be remembered for his work at Newcastle Central, was commissioned to prepare a design.

All seemed to be going well for Carlisle's two pioneer railways but subsequent events proved that the M&C, at least, had made some poor appointments to its staff. One of the high prices it eventually had to pay for

this was the rejection of the Bill for its new station and access thereto when this was submitted in the 1843 session of Parliament. Failure to comply with some of the technical formalities meant that the measure had to be resubmitted in 1844, by which time the railway scene at Carlisle had acquired a new dimension and what should have been a simple, sensible development was to turn into a *cause célèbre*.

The new dimension had first assumed a tangible shape at a meeting in Lancaster Town Hall on 12 April 1836 when the idea of a railway from Lancaster to Carlisle received considerable support. Work was already in hand on a line to Preston, and the Lancaster & Preston Junction company was planning to carry the idea of rail communication further north still. The Lancaster & Carlisle project was one of three rival schemes studied by Parliament when, in response to an address moved in the Commons on 14 August 1839, it appointed two commissioners to examine the merits of each. The two - Lt Col Sir Frederic Smith and Professor Peter Barlow - rejected the idea of a coastal route and recommended a combination of the two inland routes, using the Lancaster-Kendal section of one and the Lune Valley portion of the other.

The Smith-Barlow route was broadly the basis of the Lancaster & Carlisle Railway Act of 6 June 1844. This provided for a Carlisle station north of the eventual Citadel site, with access to the N&C's London Road until the position with the embryo Caledonian Railway became clearer. The fact that the legislators had the L&C's proposals before them in 1844, as well as the delayed M&C station scheme, resulted in the latter being saddled with a clause preventing the extension to Crown Street being made without the agreement of the Lancaster & Carlisle, unless it could be achieved without detriment to the latter's access plans.

The Lancaster & Carlisle was very quick off the mark and was cutting the first sod in the month following its Act. Difficulty was experienced in raising the £800,000 capital authorised, but the companies associated with the southern end of the emerging West Coast Main Line - the London & Birmingham, Grand Junction, North Union and Lancaster & Preston Junction - came up with help to the tune of £470,000, which enabled construction work to continue. The first section of the new railway was opened between Lancaster and Oxenholme on 22 September 1846 and the remainder on 16 December, public services through to Carlisle commencing on the following day.

Although Dobson had completed the design work for the M&C station at Crown Street, he advised the company against building it until the position regarding the Lancaster line's access and its plans for connection with the Caledonian became clearer. The M&C directors accepted this advice and modified their hopes by announcing and commencing a temporary station on the Crown Street site. A relatively simple affair, the new station was completed quickly and brought into use on 30 December 1844. Trains reached it by heading through Bogfield towards London Road, then revers-

ing into the terminus. The engines would then run round their train and propel it out at departure time, passing over the junction points and then setting off in the right direction and order.

As the Caledonian Railway Bill made its way through Parliament the question of a single, central, jointly-used station became a real issue. The site at Court Square was chosen at a meeting of all four interested parties on 24 July 1845, but the terms governing participation proved more difficult, for both the existing companies felt that the expenditure they had already incurred should be taken into account. In the case of the Maryport & Carlisle, this embraced the whole of the Crown Street site, some of which was likely to be needed for the new station. There was nearly a year of negotiation before an agreement was signed endorsing the idea in principle and agreeing that the Board of Trade should arbitrate over any disagreements in implementation or settlement.

The plans for the new layout were published in October 1846 and provided, sensibly, for the M&C goods depot to be located west of the future main line from the south, with the N&C and L&C goods facilities east thereof and on Crown Street land. More difficulties were raised, especially by the M&C, which still saw itself as a natural extension of the Newcastle line and did not relish being dominated by the north-south parties to the detriment of good east-west links. The arguments dragged on for so long that the Lancaster & Carlisle and Caledonian companies eventually decided that they had no option but to go ahead on their own, hoping that the other two would join in later.

The Act authorising the new Citadel station had been secured on 27 July 1846, relying on the original multi-railway consensus of 1845. By September a contract for the work had been let thanks largely to the energy of the Lancaster & Carlisle and the backing of its southern partners. That company's trains started using the new, albeit uncompleted, station from 1 September 1847, with the first Caledonian trains arriving from Beattock nine days later. With the M&C still using Crown Street, the new layout

Sir William Tite's Tudor-style frontage for Carlisle Citadel station.
Two of the coat-of-arms panels are blank, supposedly left for the dilatory N&C and M&C partners.

The up main platform at Carlisle Citadel station in the early years of the century. *Lens of Sutton*

meant that trains from the south twice crossed the approach line to that station, itself reached by the reversing process described earlier. Such conflicting movements were barely tolerable even in this early period of light traffic, and clearly could not survive in the long term.

As the Carlisle situation moved nearer to conflict, a new dimension appeared. The long arm of George Hudson, the so-called 'Railway King', suddenly made itself felt when the York, Newcastle & Berwick Railway, of which Hudson was the chairman, leased first the Newcastle & Carlisle then the Maryport & Carlisle; the former joined the Hudson empire from 1 August 1848 and the Maryport company from 1 October. What he wanted with these two concerns is not clear, but the Caledonian, which by now was running through to Glasgow. had tried to acquire the route to Newcastle earlier that year, and this may have been Hudson's response; he might also have seen in the

Crown Street situation an opportunity for profit and the prospect of holding the West Coast Main Line to ransom. Whatever the reason, the development boded no good for the Lancaster & Carlisle.

This prognosis was dramatically proven when Hudson demanded £100,000 for Crown Street against the sum of £7,005 that had been offered by the Lancaster & Carlisle. The long-suffering L&C now had no alternative but to turn to its Parliamentary power of acquisition of the site and accordingly placed the matter before a special jury early in 1849. At a two-day hearing in January before Coroner Carrick, the L&C representatives put their case clearly and simply while their opponents invested the matter with great drama, numerous 'expert' witnesses and the plea that M&C trains might have to revert to using Bogfield with disastrous effects upon the company's traffic levels - this and the alleged high value of the Crown Street site being used to justify the vast sum that the

At the north end of the old Crown Street site, the up bay at Carlisle is pictured here accommodating empty stock and a rake of Class '08' shunters.

company claimed. Unimpressed by all these fireworks, the court decided that the M&C must give up the Crown Street site on payment of the sum of £7,171 4s 3d, an amount the L&C immediately paid into the Bank of England to the credit of its fractious neighbour.

Through Mr Blenkinsopp of Swift & Co, the L&C's solicitors, a formal request was then made to the Maryport & Carlisle to release the Crown Street site. Mr Heysham, a director of the M&C, refused, leaving the L&C no alternative but to refer the whole matter to Carlisle's High Sheriff. That gentleman, too, had had enough of the M&C's antics, and issued orders to his Under Sheriff, L. Harrison of Penrith, that were to bring the long-simmering conflict to a dramatic head.

On the morning of Saturday 17 March 1849 Crown Street was enjoying a quiet period after the morning train had come and gone. Only the clerks were on duty and they sat in the single wooden building accounting for their paper ticket issues, keeping their records of wagons received and forwarded and generally making good use of the quiet period before the next train was due just before midday. Then, to disturb this uncomplicated scene, came the noise of a chaise coming in through the main gate and the sound of people alighting, the coach door closing and footsteps ascending the approach ramp and continuing towards the office.

The unexpected arrivals were an impressive bunch, the Under Sheriff at their head and with him lawyer Blenkinsopp and Mr Worthington, the resident engineer of the Lancaster & Carlisle company. On alighting from his vehicle, Harrison went first to the station office and advised the bemused clerks of his errand, following this by crossing the platform, then descending to track level and declaring that he gave formal possession of the site to the Lancaster & Carlisle company. At this point Worthington moved to a prominent position and waived his handkerchief, the signal for some 150 labourers from the Citadel station job to leave their assembly point in the L&C goods yard and rush over to Crown Street. All the entrances to the station were sealed by Superintendent

Bibby of the Lancaster & Carlisle company's police.

With gusto, or 'con amore' as the Carlisle Patriot put it, the invaders set to work on the wooden platforms, ripping the joints apart and piling the wood nearby. They levered up the rails from their host sleepers, then moved on to the coal and lime depot track and buildings, putting horses and drag chains to work on any particularly obstinate piece of M&C hardware. Some sections needed the combined efforts of 50-60 men, but the demolition work was not allowed to flag and provided much to amaze the sizeable crowd of spectators who could hardly have expected so much entertainment on a conventional Saturday morning. Watching all this but hardly able to believe their eyes, the bemused clerks were next told to gather up their books and leave, and no sooner had they done so than the demolition teams went to work on the main station building, quickly bringing this down and loading the debris into carts to carry it away.

Superintendent Bibby had also posted a man at the rail approach to Crown Street station to warn the driver of the train due at 11.30 am. What that worthy must have thought when advised that he could not proceed as his destination had been knocked down is not recorded. At any event he took his train to London Road instead and all its passengers suffered was a somewhat longer walk into town. There, handbills confirmed that the days of Crown Street station were over and future services would use the N&C station.

As the dust settled on the Crown Street site, so the recriminations began. Hudson's own downfall meant that there was little point in pursuing him, and the M&C directors had no choice but to resume control of their own operations from 1 January 1850. They took the Lancaster & Carlisle to court, but lost the case when the 1846 agreement was held to have remained valid. With the shareholders getting increasingly vociferous, the M&C directors then sought to make a scapegoat of the company's solicitor, G. G. Mounsey, but this move also rebounded when that gentleman gathered a group

Two views of part of the Crown Street station area at the London end of Carlisle Citadel station, showing the L&C bridge over Crown Street itself from Citadel station and from road level.

around him and demanded a full enquiry into the affairs and management of the company. A Committee of Investigation was appointed and went on to reveal an incredible state of irregularity and mismanagement among the M&C's domestic affairs. The situation became almost laughable when Hudson submitted a claim for compensation over the Crown Street affair, alleging that he had been misinformed!

Sanity had to reassert itself, and eventually changes in the Maryport & Carlisle's board of directors brought common sense to bear. Agreement was reached with the L&C for the use of Citadel, based on an annual rental plus a share of the working expenses, and trains from Maryport started running into the

joint station from 1 June 1851. Initially the M&C services had to continue their old reversing habit, but Parliamentary authority was obtained for a direct link from Bogfield to simplify the access from 8 August 1852.

Citadel finally fulfilled its builders' intentions when it absorbed the London Road passenger services at the beginning of 1863. By then it was also being used by the Glasgow & South Western services and those on the newly opened Border Union line. Only the Settle & Carlisle trains were still to come, and these duly arrived on 1 May 1876; soon afterwards the approach layout was remodelled to abolish the highly-inconvenient level crossings, and the station considerably enlarged from its original single-platform state. The

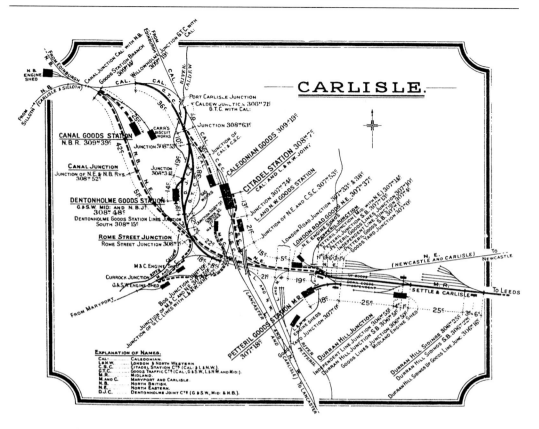

The railways of Carlisle in 1914, as shown in the Midland Railway Distance Diagrams,
showing the curve allowing the M&C direct access to Citadel station from Bogfield (Currock Junction).

enlargement added £379,135 to the original cost of £180,000, but the result was a station that remains impressive even now.

The West Coast Main Line today enters Citadel station over an alignment slightly to the west of its Lancaster & Carlisle ancestor. After the junctions with the old M&C and N&C routes it passes above Crown Street via an ornamental bridge to reach the station's main down island. Down at road level the former Crown Street site, part of which was occupied by the LNWR goods depot from 1867, is now marked by modern commercial buildings at one end and the up station bay at the other. At road level Crown Street itself, and the adjoining Collier Lane, still have something of the atmosphere of times past, but today's observer would be hard put to imagine the scenes of 17 March 1849 as reported by the *Illustrated London News* under the dramatic heading 'A Railway Station Taken by Storm'.

5
RIVAL INTERESTS AT CHESTER

From 1838 passengers were able to travel between London and the North West over the lines of the London & Birmingham Railway and its northern partner the Grand Junction Railway. However, in an age that abhorred monopoly and in which demand for passenger and goods movement had already been stimulated by the canals, it was not to be expected that the new lines, important as they were, would remain the only trunk rail route to the rich industries of Lancashire and their great port on the Mersey. Conscious of this, the partners in the new main line were constantly watchful, encouraging schemes likely to contribute traffic to their own metals, opposing those that might threaten them and trying to ensure that each secured no advantage over the other.

In such a situation it is hardly surprising that conflicts should emerge, but out of this particular situation were to come three major confrontations, the growth of a bitter enmity between two great railways and the creation of a new route to the Mersey. The first of the confrontations was to take place at Chester.

As part of the process of creating its own sphere of influence, the Grand Junction Railway gave active support to the Chester & Crewe Railway, a local scheme that was authorised to build a 21¼-mile line between those two places on 30 June 1837. Indeed, the GJR took over the smaller company just three months before the latter's opening on 1 October 1840, and later planned to use it as a springboard for access to Ireland via Holyhead. A second railway authorised in

Protagonists:
Shrewsbury & Chester Railway and London & North Western Railway

Location:
Chester station

Date:
8 November 1849 and subsequently

1837 (12 July) also reached Chester in 1840. This was the Chester & Birkenhead, which opened from Grange Lane to Chester on 23 September 1840 and also had strong connections with the GJR.

Meanwhile, not relishing its dependence on the Grand Junction, the London & Birmingham was showing interest in other schemes involving the Welsh border counties. It encouraged the embryo Shrewsbury & Birmingham and Chester & Holyhead railway schemes, both of which emerged from a period of trade depression at the beginning of the 1840s with considerable enthusiasm and impetus. The Chester & Holyhead, with Government support, got its enabling Act on 4 July 1844 and was encouraged by the L&B to think of a link southwards to Shrewsbury as an alternative to the Grand Junction outlet via Crewe. All these influences, coupled with the domestic railway ambitions of

Shrewsbury, Wrexham and Chester, were fuelling the case for a new trunk railway that would serve these places on its way to North Wales and the Mersey.

The first practical step came when the North Wales Mineral Railway was empowered to construct a railway from Wrexham to Saltney, there to join the Chester & Holyhead and use the latter's metals for the last few miles into Chester. The NWMR Act of 6 August 1844 was followed on 30 June 1845 by the authorisation of a Shrewsbury-Ruabon line to the Shrewsbury, Oswestry & Chester Junction Railway and, on 21 July 1845, of a line to fill the Wrexham-Ruabon gap, to the North Wales Mineral company. By this time work on the section north of Wrexham was well advanced and there was talk of amalgamation between the two local concerns, which had the common objective of thwarting the Shrewsbury ambitions of the Chester & Holyhead Railway.

The year 1845 also heralded the beginning of drama on the wider stage. First the Manchester & Birmingham Railway, long fretting over its dependence on the Grand Junction, amalgamated with the London & Birmingham, then all three came together from the beginning of 1846 to form the London & North Western Railway, a new and powerful grouping that certainly wanted no new route to the Mersey unless it could acquire or dominate it.

But things had gone too far for the withdrawal of L&B support to deter the smaller companies it had once encouraged. By an Act of 27 July 1846 the lines between Chester and Shrewsbury were amalgamated as the Shrewsbury & Chester Railway, with the companion Shrewsbury & Birmingham enterprise receiving the Royal Assent on 3 August of the same year to complete the authorities necessary for a through line from Birmingham to Birkenhead. Other Parliamentary activity in 1846 included authorisation of a joint station at Shrewsbury and of the Birkenhead, Lancashire & Cheshire Junction Railway. The latter added a Warrington line to the existing one from Chester to Birkenhead, which was absorbed into the new BL&CJ company on 22 July

1847. The newly created Shrewsbury & Chester opened its (mainly single) line from Ruabon to Saltney on 4 November 1846, and its trains were able to continue into Chester thanks to an agreement under which the Chester & Holyhead completed the difficult works on this section ahead of the rest of its route.

It was clear that the original station at Chester would be inadequate once the lines to Shrewsbury and Holyhead were completed. Accordingly Parliamentary approval was secured on 9 July 1847 for the building of a new station that would be managed jointly by the participating railways. The management committee was to be made up of

two LNWR directors with three votes,
two Chester & Holyhead directors with three votes,
two Shrewsbury & Chester directors with two votes, and
two BL&CJ directors with two votes

who would appoint a station manager for day-to-day running.

The design of the new station was put in the hands of Francis Thompson, and the construction work entrusted to local boy Thomas Brassey, who got on with the task quickly and had the works completed in time for opening on 1 August 1848. Behind a dramatic 1,050-feet frontage lay a long main departure platform with bays at each end for the arriving services. The main block included separate booking office accommodation for the four constituent partners, and each company had administrative offices along the upper storey. Opening was none too soon, for Chester & Holyhead services had begun running to and from Bangor on 1 May 1848 (worked by the LNWR), and S&C trains started working through from Shrewsbury on 14 October. The revenue from the latter and the sharing of station expenses was a relief to the ambitious S&C, which had already decided to subscribe £75,000 to the Shrewsbury & Hereford scheme to widen its outlets.

With construction work on the line from Shrewsbury to Wolverhampton being pushed

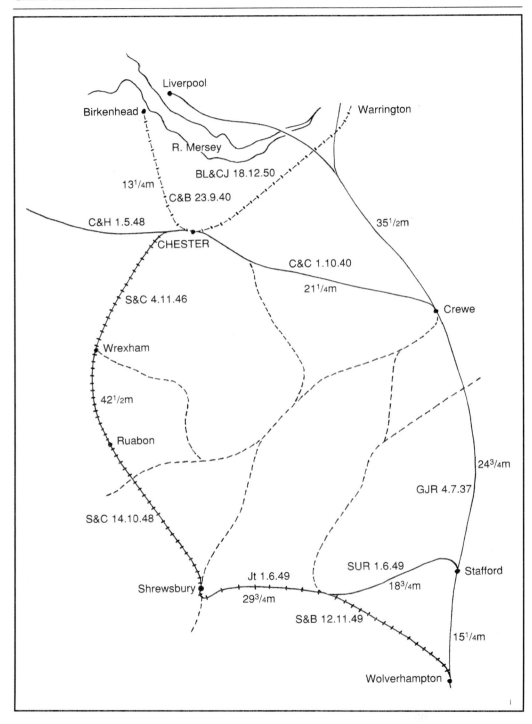

Railways around Chester, showing their opening dates.

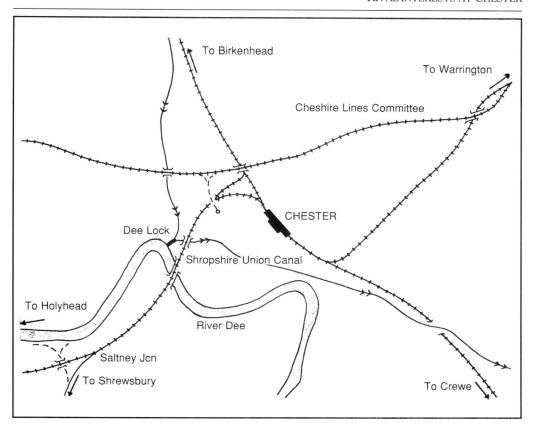

The railways and waterways of Chester.

The magnificent frontage of Chester station is slightly marred by the paraphernalia of improvements being carried out in 1993. Today's buses find no hindrance to their access to the premises, unlike their 1849 counterparts!

ahead, the two Shrewsbury companies set up a joint traffic committee, which quickly saw that neither line was going to prosper on purely local traffic. What was needed was through traffic passing over the whole length of the route, and especially a share of the lucrative business of the port of Liverpool. The next step was an approach to the Birkenhead company proposing tripartite action, including the offer of lower fares to compensate for passengers having to cross the Mersey.

The Chester & Birkenhead had experienced problems with the Grand Junction Railway right from opening, the latter putting every possible obstacle in the way of traffic routed via Chester as an alternative to its own direct route from the Mersey. To cater for the expanded docks activity at Liverpool and Birkenhead, the company had extended from Grange Lane to Rock Ferry on 23 October 1844 and, after passing to the Birkenhead, Lancashire & Cheshire Junction concern, added a second track to the previous single line from Chester to Birkenhead. Disputes at the Mersey end had kept the Birkenhead concern poor, and it could less easily afford to offend the GJC and its LNWR successor than the two Shrewsbury companies, who believed that they had everything to gain and little to lose.

Initially the BL&CJ responded positively to the S&C/S&B rates proposals, but then the LNWR got to hear of the matter and expressed itself in no uncertain terms. An ultimatum was delivered to the S&C in October 1849, the month before the Shrewsbury & Birmingham was due to open. In it Mark Huish wrote:

'It is stated by the Shrewsbury & Birmingham Company that you are about to join them in opposing us, at low rates, between Birkenhead and Wolverhampton, and thence by coach to Birmingham for passengers, and by canal for goods; will you tell me candidly whether this is the case? I trust not, and that your Company and ours may avoid the competition which has brought so much loss to other parties.

I need not say that if you should be unwise enough to encourage such a proceeding, it must result in a general fight both by our railway from Shrewsbury to Liverpool and by our Shropshire Canal, the only gainers being of course the public and the Shrewsbury & Birmingham Company. Let me hope, however, that there is no truth in the statements; or, if there is, that you will reconsider your measures.

Yours truly
Mark Huish'

The recipient of this letter, Robert Roy, was not a man to be intimidated by the LNWR, or anyone else. Indeed, it later became clear that one of his own chairmen had quit because he felt that Roy exercised too much influence over the company's directors. Be that as it may, Roy's response to Mark Huish on 18 October was wordy but uncompromising:

'. . .This Company have always looked for a share of the through traffic on the opening of the lines to the south of Shrewsbury; the small difference in the length of the two lines making it a matter of course. It is a part, we think, of our legitimate traffic. It is intended to carry through passengers only, first, second and third class, at reduced rates with our regular trains; the extent of the reduction will depend on the arrangements of your Company. For the present we look to 30 or 40 per cent, and you will be aware that as the addition of a few through carriages to our local trains occasions scarcely any expense, a much greater reduction would leave a handsome profit.

As to goods, you will learn from Mr Skey that you are misinformed, this Company being prepared either to continue or give up the amicable arrangements with your Shropshire Union ally, which have been acted upon since the first opening of the line. Indeed, our refusal to break off those arrangements with them was assigned by the

Birkenhead Company as the leading reason for declining to accept a mileage proportion of the through traffic instead of their ordinary fares, a matter of too small amount on their short length to affect so large a question in one way or other, although it and other considerations may deprive them permanently of our goods traffic, and place it on the Shropshire Union Canal into Liverpool; or, according to circumstances, by the Dee steamers to Liverpool, as the Runcorn trade is carried on. But altho' perfectly prepared to compete with you or them for whatever traffic we are entitled to, our Directors are equally prepared to arrange the whole questions that may arise, or any part of them separately by itself, on proper and reasonable terms.

I have thought it right to give you this explicit intimation of our views and position, and our disposition to arrange, in consequence of the terms of your letter - written, I have no doubt, in the hurry of business - in order that you may be perfectly aware that if a 'general fight', as you express it, arise, it is not of our seeking, nor from any unreasonable views on the part of this Company.'

Following this forthright rejection of the LNWR threats, the Shrewsbury & Chester then found that the other company, by using its hold over the Chester & Holyhead to create a majority on the Chester station committee, had stopped the booking of local passengers via Shrewsbury. The S&C booking clerk was ejected from his office, his tickets and papers thrown out after him and the door locked to prevent re-entry. Frightened off by this strong-arm stuff, the Birkenhead repudiated its agreement with the Shrewsbury companies and followed the LNWR example in putting obstacles in their path. Through fares via Shrewsbury were withdrawn and trains retimed to worsen the connections, so that travellers south from Monks Ferry and the Birkenhead line stations found it easier to travel on via Crewe than via Shrewsbury.

From 1 June 1849 the matter had been getting increasingly serious for the Shrewsbury railways, for on that day the S&B and Shropshire Union opened their joint line from Shrewsbury to Wellington and S&B trains were able to work as far as Oakengates. From 12 November they would be continuing on to a temporary station at Wolverhampton. The rival interests were all aware of the situation further ahead when passengers would be able to travel on to Birmingham, then choose between the former L&B route and that of the GWR via Snow Hill and the Oxford line. These were exciting prospects, and the Shrewsbury companies were in no mood to be excluded from them. If the Birkenhead company was too timid for these heady affairs, the Shrewsbury partners would go ahead without them!

The first move in the Chester battle proper occurred at the beginning of November 1849 when the Secretary of the Shrewsbury & Chester Railway advised Mr Jones, the station manager at Chester, that they would need facilities for a new omnibus service that was to operate from Monday the 5th. The requirement was for watering and feed facilities plus a spot to load and discharge passengers and shelter for waiting drivers. The S&C gave no indication as to its precise intentions, and Mr Jones, helpfully but innocently, responded with a proposal to charge 1s 6d per vehicle and a proviso that he would need to consult the station committee. In fact, the S&C plan was to do something practical about the failure of the Birkenhead line to provide reasonable through fares and convenient connections. Taking matters into its own hands, the S&C intended to bring Mersey passengers to Chester by laying on an omnibus service and had gone to a Mr Smith, one of the local omnibus proprietors, to arrange the necessary vehicles.

The new arrangements worked well for the first three days, just about the time it would take for the LNWR agent to apprise Euston of the development and get a reaction back again. By the Thursday, the S&C's opponents had marshalled themselves, decided upon their course of action and even warned the local constabulary that there could be

The Birkenhead (right) and Holyhead/Shrewsbury routes separate at the country end of Chester station.

trouble. On the Thursday morning the station manager also warned the omnibus drivers that they would no longer be allowed on the station premises 'for the purpose of decoying passengers from using the Birkenhead line.' He clearly meant the threat, for when the unlucky Driver Worthington, an employee of the omnibus firm, drove his horse bus to the designated loading point at the station, he found that a barrier had been erected to deny him access and the area was thronged with people. In addition to a group of policemen, each of the four Chester railways had its porters out in strength, while on the tracks nearby the LNWR adherents had 'a train filled with navvies armed with clubs' who, the *Chester Chronicle* maintained, 'had arrived ready for any work which might be apportioned to them.'

Despite the warning not to enter the station, Driver Worthington was not a man of faint heart and responded by trying to drive round the barrier. The constabulary fell upon him and before an S&C protest could be mounted they had the unfortunate fellow under lock and key. S&C staff, with no one to fight for, were hustled back to their normal duties and the LNWR 'army' hauled away from the trouble zone, but not before the S&C's timebills and posters had been thoroughly vandalised.

The main victim of the incident, Driver Worthington, was left to spend a night in the lock-up, then to appear in court on the following day. There he was charged with wilfully impeding the business of the station in an action brought by station manager Jones and defended by the S&C. The former argued that the station regulations precluded any company from operating buses over the routes of the others, and the latter that the 'arrest' was made without any reference to the station committee and that, in any event, full access was within the S&C's rights. The magistrates, wisely perhaps, decided that the matter was not for them and refused to try it. Driver Worthington was released and faded from the scene, no doubt well pleased to be out of it.

In the Vice Chancellor's Court on Tuesday 4 December the S&C appeared seeking an injunction against the others. The company sought free access to the station at Chester, maintaining that this was clearly their right and that the actions of the other users in stopping them was all part of a plan, orchestrated by the LNWR, to strangle the smaller concern. The response of the latter was to reveal that the station committee had already debated the matter on 3 November when the S&C had been outvoted and a resolution made that each railway should only use omnibuses in proportion to its overall activities.

Sir J. K. Bruce, after considering the representations made by counsel and witnesses for the opposing parties, took much the same view as the magistrates and declared that he could decide only upon the immediate facts without going into the background politics. He did, however, rule that the Shrewsbury & Chester should have its booking facilities back, but only on a basis approved by the other partners. This limitation was then overturned on appeal to the Lord Chancellor.

It seems that the Chester events were repeated at Monks Ferry for the *Chester Chronicle* added to its report of 16 November:

'In consequence of the disagreement between the above-named companies, the spirit exhibited at our station was manifested simultaneously at Birkenhead. It appears that the omnibuses before starting from Birkenhead were usually driven to the Monk's Ferry station to pick up passengers. On Thursday, the driver was ordered away and, refusing to obey the order, he was taken into custody, and the following morning brought before the Birkenhead magistrates who refused to adjudicate in the case. . .'

An uneasy truce lasted until April of the following year when the next move of the LNWR was to persuade the Birkenhead to withdraw all through facilities with the S&C in return for a receipts guarantee. On 4 April the S&C was advised of the Birkenhead company's new policy and for six months confusion reigned, with passengers forced to rebook, goods sent by incredibly circuitous routes including the use of canals and of steamers on the Dee, and the Chester-Birkenhead omnibuses operating fully loaded. When the S&C threatened to apply for running powers over the Birkenhead line there was a revolt by the shareholders of the BL&JC company, which ended this phase of hostility for a short period.

The year 1851 started off no better that its predecessors, with a row over the S&C's use of the BL&CJ's Warrington line for getting traffic to Manchester. The LNWR maintained that its agreement with the Birkenhead did not extend to S&C traffic, which must be transhipped! The S&C response was to invite the Birkenhead company to join the alliance planned with the Great Western, making that company feel all the more harassed. When the invitation was backed up with an S&C threat of an Act for replacing previous agreements with actual running powers from Saltney to Chester and over the Birkenhead lines, the BL&CJ shareholders began to see where their best advantage lay.

These developments rekindled the main conflict with the LNWR, which was not without its supporters in the S&C ranks. Matters erupted at a company meeting on Thursday 12 June when the GWR amalgamation item was pushed off the agenda by the LNWR party's suggestion that a better deal might be available, a proposal which they backed with a trainload of supporters! A compromise was reached on the following day based on putting off the main issue in order to secure the 80 per cent support necessary for the Birkenhead Bill. This was implemented on Wednesday 18 June, but not before both parties had begun a pamphlet war in readiness for the resumption of discussions on the main GWR question on 16 July.

The directors' pamphlet came out with some startling accusations, maintaining that of 208 share transfers sent in after 9 June, 144 of the parties named lived within one mile of Euston or Camden! On the 9th the opposition was said to have lodged transfers for 4,500 £10 shares (on which only £1 was paid), split into 32 lots to give the highest voting power. Not to be outdone, the LNWR party maintained that the directors had created 400 shareholders and 6-8,000 votes by splitting existing holdings. They quoted examples of two Edinburgh shareholders and one in Romford whose holdings had been used to create 3,642 additional votes!

The rebel leader, a Mr Thompson, was peddling an LNWR takeover offer backed by a receipts guarantee, and the loyal directors were forced to defend themselves and their GWR plans at a series of shareholders' meetings throughout the country. The tension was rising steadily and all the arguments and frustrations came to a head at the resumed meeting at the Royal Hotel Assembly Rooms on 16 July. The meeting started with an attempt to read a letter from the Great Western in which it promised to reach Birmingham in eight months and to establish a connection with the Shrewsbury companies via the Oxford, Worcester & Wolverhampton Railway. 'Confusion and uproar' were the order of the day as the opening speaker was shouted down and had to give way to another with a louder voice. Thompson called the GWR agreement 'a delusion' and got a pithy response, with some allegations about his share-dealing and a measure of sly 'nodding and winking' from Mr Roy. As the *Chronicle* described the subsequent events:

'. . .amidst the most tremendous uproar . . .the appearance of Mr Gotch and a gentleman in the body of the room violently gesticulating and apparently energetically declaiming at one another, although it was impossible for either to hear a sound. . .was irresistibly ludicrous.'

Then Roy got to his feet and presented the facts behind the original meeting, confirming that the LNWR was using one of its old tactics of buying up shares to acquire votes for its viewpoint. He said that

'. . .it was necessary to make them acquainted with some of the methods of warfare which had been practised against the Company and the directors. Information reached the Board on 6th June that a mass of £10 shares had been eagerly collected in Liverpool by parties connected with the London & North Western Company. Considering what this might augur the directors came to the conclusion that the shares had been purchased to be used against themselves and other bona fide shareholders since altho' they were £10 shares, £1 only was paid in full. They therefore determined to take such precautionary measures as would prevent the bona fide interests being swamped at the meeting and of defending themselves if anything unfair were attempted. On examining the mass of transfers submitted for registration just before the meeting on 12th June it was found that there was no less than 140 of 32 shares each, making up about 2,000 votes, the whole of which were plainly lodged for the purpose of swamping the meeting.'

The S&C secretary went on to reveal that the transfers had originally been in the names of the LNWR manager and secretary (Huish and Stewart), and made light of the company's use of the same ploy to counter its enemy. He also managed to withdraw, but not retract, his 'severe epithets' about Mr Thompson. Although the tellers were not able to complete their count that evening because the noise, argument and abuse was near continuous, at 11 am on the following morning it revealed a massive 17,831 in favour of the GWR tie-up and only 7,040 for the LNWR offer.

In October 1851 the BL&CJ came back into the Shrewsbury fold and joined in the alliance with the GWR, but then found that, in the following year, the LNWR was putting forward a Bill for its own line to Birkenhead. Another change of heart followed and at the end of 1852 the S&C was presented with demands for a massive increase in charges for operating through to Birkenhead. Legislation was resorted to, but technically the BL&CJ was within its rights and could charge up to the legal maximum. Again the S&C proved a match for its opponents by offering the traffic at Chester and, since its volume was too high for the BL&CJ to ignore, that company was forced to buy extra engines to work it! Other events of 1852 included a further purchase offer from the LNWR, another S&C shareholders revolt, another rejection of the GWR link, and its reversal by the main body of directors.

A few last campaigns remained to be fought to round off this five-year battle. The Birkenhead company was, in January 1854, awarded £8,500 by arbitration of its dispute with the Shrewsbury & Chester. The taxation on this sum was determined on 2 March and on that same day the BL&CJ issued writs against its neighbour that resulted in stations and property worth £50,000 being brought within the seizure process. It was held for two days, during which time S&C activities were seriously disrupted, but things returned to normal when payment was made. At this period the BL&CJ half-yearly meeting was complaining of the loss of traffic from the Duke of Bridgewater's Trustees as a result of 'powers granted to the S&C to carry across

the Mersey and then diverted from the LNW by carrying it on to Norton for transhipment and rail carriage south, depriving the BL&C of four miles of tolls and terminal charges.'

Later that year the S&C, now firmly within the GWR camp, secured Parliamentary reinforcement of its running powers over the Birkenhead lines, and that concern's long-suffering shareholders finally decided that enough was enough and ousted the LNWR-lovers on its board. Peace for Chester at last.

Chester station today seems an unlikely place for the startling events of Thursday 8 November 1849. The 320-metre frontage remains handsome and imposing, but its rooms are no longer occupied by four rival railways and the only buses in evidence are those of the very useful service into the heart of the historic city. The station layout was, in fact, changed dramatically in 1890 when a large island was added outside the original main platform, but the bay used by the Shrewsbury trains is still in action today. A plaque on the station commemorates Thomas Brassey, but there is no memorial to Driver Worthington or any other of the stalwarts who were determined not to be trampled underfoot by the might of the London & North Western company.

Chester station, with the original platform and Shrewsbury bay on the right and the later island, with a 'Sprinter' unit, on the left.

6
WOLVERHAMPTON:
THE FIRST CONFLICT

One of the longest and most bitter battles of railway history centred upon Wolverhampton. That city derived its first railway service from a station (later called Wednesfield Heath) on the Grand Junction's 1837 trunk line to the north, but the demands of the growing local population and business activity required something better than this, and the rush to fill the vacuum produced a period of obstruction and attrition that is without parallel in the picturesque annals of railway rivalry.

A principal player in the drama was the Shrewsbury & Birmingham Railway, formed in 1844 as the Shrewsbury & Wolverhampton, Dudley & Birmingham Railway, which was quickly offered a lease by the influential London & Birmingham Railway as part of its quest for a route to the Mersey that would lessen its dependence on the Grand Junction company. As outlined in the previous chapter, these two, although partners in the trunk rail route from Euston to the North West, distrusted one another thoroughly and quarrelled violently over both the L&B's Trent Valley scheme and the GJR's rival plans for Shrewsbury. Their attitude changed dramatically from 1846 when they became partners in the mighty London & North Western Railway, which was soon to become the bitterest enemy of the tiny Shrewsbury & Birmingham concern.

Raising the temperature of local rivalries was the development of the larger railway picture in which the Great Western featured prominently. The GWR had taken over the

| Protagonists: |
| Shrewsbury & Birmingham Railway and London & North Western Railway |
| **Location:** |
| North of Wolverhampton High Level station |
| **Date:** |
| 12 and 13 July 1850 |

GJR interest in the Birmingham & Oxford Railway and could reach Wolverhampton over the Birmingham, Wolverhampton & Dudley Railway once these two lines were completed. Previously at loggerheads with the London & Birmingham, the GWR now became a threat to the LNWR conglomerate, and local companies were not slow to see advantage in alliances with one party or the other as their rival positions steadily grew stronger.

The B&O and BW&D Acts were passed on 3 August 1846, with the local Shrewsbury & Birmingham Railway being authorised on the same day. After the failure of the original S&WD&B scheme as a result of Grand Junction opposition, the idea had been revived as the Shrewsbury & Birmingham Railway project. Parliamentary committee activity then hived off the section south of Wolverhampton to a separate company, the Birmingham, Wolverhampton & Stour

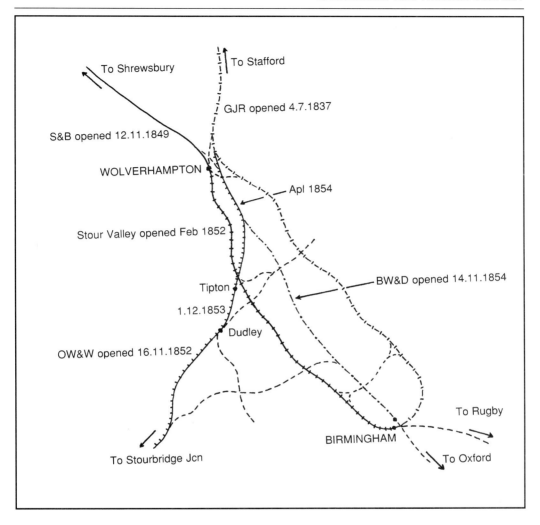

To Stafford

To Shrewsbury

GJR opened 4.7.1837

S&B opened 12.11.1849

WOLVERHAMPTON

Apl 1854

Stour Valley opened Feb 1852

Tipton

BW&D opened 14.11.1854

1.12.1853

Dudley

OW&W opened 16.11.1852

To Rugby

BIRMINGHAM

To Stourbridge Jcn

To Oxford

Early lines between Wolverhampton and Birmingham.

Valley Railway, in which the S&B had a quarter interest, along with the Birmingham Canal Company and the London & North Western, public subscription accounting for the remaining fourth share. At the Shrewsbury end of the line there was a further price to pay for placating the opposition, in that the 10 miles to Wellington was authorised to the S&B as a joint operation with the Shropshire Union Railways & Canal Company, which had sought authority for a railway from Shrewsbury to Stafford.

The distant rumble of conflict thunder was brought nearer by an agreement between the LNWR and the Birmingham Canal under which the former could exercise control when it was called upon to underwrite the canal system's earnings. This gave the railway a strong influence on the latter's quarter share in the Stour Valley company, and led to the LNWR proposing to lease that company, along with the Shropshire Union. The S&B opposed this step initially, but withdrew its objection after negotiations in 1847 that established a pooling agreement for traffic on the joint line, protected it against diversions

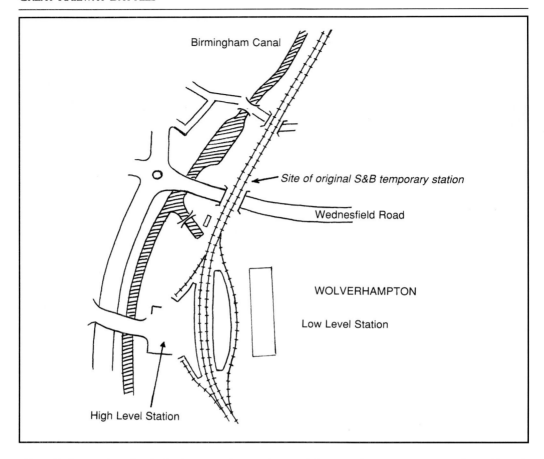

Birmingham Canal

Site of original S&B temporary station

Wednesfield Road

WOLVERHAMPTON

Low Level Station

High Level Station

Above Railway and canal at Wolverhampton, showing the site of the original S&B terminus at Wednesfield Road.

Above right The canal and the railway are still neighbours at Wolverhampton. This view, looking north, shows Wednesfield Road crossing the Birmingham Canal on the left, and the platforms of the High Level station on the extreme right.

Right A closer view of the northern approaches to Wolverhampton, just to the right of the previous photograph, as an up InterCity service arrives at the High Level station. The bridge parapet visible on the left is that spanning Wednesfield Road.

via Stafford and gave the S&B formal running powers over the future Stour Valley route between Wolverhampton and Birmingham. It is revealing of the LNWR's fears that these powers were conditional upon the S&B not being leased to the Great Western or amalgamated with the GWR or its associates.

A further agreement between the S&B and LNW concerns, also ratified by an Act of July 1847, provided for a joint permanent station at Wolverhampton and, since each had powers to build the section of line between there and the point of divergence between the Shrewsbury and Stafford lines, for this short length to become joint also. Its running would be in the hands of a committee of three directors from each of the two railways. Despite the apparent protection of these various agreements, the S&B was now involved with the large and ruthless LNWR system at each end of its line. Not a good augury.

It took the Shrewsbury & Birmingham nearly a year to acquire the land it required and let the various construction contracts, but 1848 was a year of better progress and by the beginning of 1849 the project was sufficiently advanced for station building to begin. Soon the long-cherished hopes of the proprietors were to become a reality as the first section of line, from Wellington to Oakengates, was opened on 1 June. The Shrewsbury-Wellington section, joint with the Shropshire Union company, was brought into use on the same day, but access to Wolverhampton was held up pending completion of Oakengates Tunnel. Eventually this, too, was finished and the route extended to a temporary station adjoining Wednesfield Road at Wolverhampton on 12 November. To celebrate the occasion a great train of 50 carriages set out from Shrewsbury at 8.30 am behind the appropriately named locomotives *Wrekin* and *Salopian*. The only cloud on the horizon was the growing tension between the Shrewsbury & Chester, with whom the S&B had a traffic agreement and a close working relationship, and the giant LNWR.

By 1850 the dispute between the S&C and LNWR companies was in full swing and began to spill over into the Shrewsbury & Birmingham domain. The LNWR started to issue cheap fares from Shrewsbury to Wolverhampton via Stafford, despite the theoretical constraints of the 1847 agreement. Immediately the S&B sought and was granted an injunction to stop this practice, but the decision was then reversed as part of a legal wrangle that was to drag on for two years, all the while contributing to the growing antagonism between the two railways.

To supplement the revenue from its nine daily passenger trains each way between Wolverhampton and Shrewsbury/Chester, the S&B was keen to attract freight business and hit on the idea of transferring consignments to the Birmingham Canal where the two systems ran alongside one another near the temporary Wolverhampton station. The line of the canal had been altered to accommodate the Stour Valley works, and it passed within a few feet of the S&B tracks at a slightly lower elevation. This was the ideal spot to transfer traffic and the directors gave authority for the construction of a wooden barrow route for discharging from railway wagon to barge.

When the S&B workmen tried to begin their construction task in April 1850 they were prevented by the Stour Valley's engineer William Baker, a former S&B and Shropshire Union man. Baker maintained that he controlled site access while work was still in progress, and that the Joint Committee's approval had not been obtained. That body, at a meeting on 7 May, remitted the matter to the respective engineers, who had their proposals ready in time for the June meeting, only to find that the Stour Valley representatives failed to turn up. However, since Mr Baker had apparently already signed the plan, the S&B authorities decided that they could begin work anyway.

By Friday 12 July 1850 workmen were busy constructing the transfer facilities, and had reached the stage of putting an access gate in the boundary fence where it ran along the rear of the canal wharf. News of this activity reached Hill & Moore, the SVR contractors, and immediately their Mr Moore set out with a gang of men to halt what he considered to be interference on his site. He announced that he could not allow the work to proceed. At this point Mr Darkin, the S&B's assistant secretary, also turned up and, relying on the trespass powers in the railway's enabling Act, asked Moore to leave.

'If you do not leave, I shall be under the necessity of giving you into custody,' was the way Darkin put it.

'You'll have to handcuff me to do it,' was Moore's defiant reply, and in that spirit he went down the bank, 'pulled the rails about', and invited his supporters to do the same.

It took all of Darkin's authority and powers of argument to put a stop to these antics and persuade the belligerent contractor that they would be better off putting the matter before the magistrates then sitting at the police court.

Legal representatives and witnesses were hastily summoned to join the process, the S&B engineer Henry Robertson maintaining that each company had a right to use the line but no right to obstruct it, and Mr Moore insisting that he could not be a trespasser on his own site. Solicitor Underhill, for the S&B, referred to the background to the matter in the following terms:

'. . .there could not be a question that the dispute arose out of the ill-feeling between the two companies. His clients wished to carry their traffic to Birmingham, which the London and North Western Company desired to prevent, and would not complete the Stour Valley line.'

More than a little perplexed by the whole business, the magistrates declined to rule or to bind Moore over to keep the peace, but they did warn him not to infringe it.

The magistrates' warning to Moore was soon proved ineffectual, for a gang of his men appeared at the dispute site early on the following day clearly determined to prevent the S&B doing any more work. When this was reported to them the S&B's traffic manager, Mr Parsons, and Henry Underhill the solicitor went to see the Wolverhampton mayor at around 9.30 and put the facts to him. They made the point that not only could they not complete delivery of the cinder traffic held in wagons awaiting transfer, but that the threats being made were very likely to lead to a breach of the peace.

His Worship was clearly a man of action and, after talks with the Chief Constable and putting the military on standby, set off for the trouble spot. Arriving there at 11.30 he was astonished to see it occupied by some 300 Stour Valley workmen all 'armed' with spades, pick-axes or other tools of their trade. Not far away was a smaller force of S&B men, clearly unhappy at being prevented from getting on with their job of building the transfer structure. Despite the mayor 'expostulating with the agents of both parties on the impropriety of bringing two bodies of men into collision when the courts of law were open to both', neither party would give way, the S&B maintaining the right of access to its own working line and pointing out, significantly, that the LNWR party had already

gone to law over the Chester situation and lost.

A new factor was now introduced to the stalemate with the arrival of an engine and wagons containing another 200 S&B men, each with his tools and each sporting a piece of red tape round his upper arm to ensure friend could be distinguished from foe. At first the two parties contented themselves with the exchange of friendly jibes, but the tension increased noticeably when the company engineer, Henry Robertson, gave orders for work to be resumed on the transfer staging. For a short period the gang delegated to do this remained unhindered, but the moment the first plank was laid up the embankment a signal was given to the Stour Valley contingent, from which a group set about throwing the planks aside. Others joined in from both sides, but eventually the smaller S&B group was overpowered, one of them sustaining a bad leg injury in the process.

Colonel Hogg, the Chief Constable, had gone for reinforcements the moment trouble seemed unavoidable, and he now returned at the head of some 50 constables, among them a number of specials sworn in for duty at the fair. Behind the police came a detachment of soldiers from the 48th Regiment commanded by Captain Sykes and advancing with bayonets fixed, much to the alarm of the spectators, many of whom felt it wise to make themselves scarce. But Moore's men were made of sterner stuff and showed no sign of budging. Confusion and danger seemed to hang in the air as the three armies confronted one another, the SVR contractors' men on the embankment, the S&B followers near their wagons and the forces of law and order waiting at the end of the platform.

Bravely the mayor placed himself at the centre of the conflict and was joined there by Mr Underhill, Colonel Hogg and a handful of policemen. Trouble seemed likely to flare up again at any moment, especially when a few S&B men made a move to resume plank-laying and Mr Knowles, who was in charge of the SVR forces, signalled his own men to cut them off. The mayor's reaction was immediate. He literally pushed Knowles and one of his followers back and, removing his hat, declared at the top of his voice:

'I am called here, as the Mayor of this borough, to prevent a breach of the peace. I see before me several hundred workmen, evidently keeping the slope of this railway to prevent some other party using it, and I also see some hundreds of workmen brought here to take possession of it. I have nothing to do with the quarrel between the parties; it is nothing to me to whom the land belongs. But the law does not permit legal rights to be decided by violence and physical force. It is not to be tolerated that hundreds of persons are to come here to assert their rights, or their imagined rights, by brute force, and so long as I am Mayor of this borough they will not do so with impunity. Even such an assemblage as this is itself illegal, and every person engaging in it is liable to be indicted. I doubt whether I ought not at once to disperse it, and I shall certainly do so unless you very soon go away of your own accord; but I hope you will not render it necessary for me to take that step, and the course which I shall at present adopt is this - I go into no questions of property. I see before me some hundred men sitting peaceably under an assertion of right by Messrs Hill and Moore, their employers. I shall not allow them to be disturbed, and if any person on the opposite side does attempt by force to remove them I will immediately commit him. I see on the other side of me a large number of men [S&B men who had now taken up their former work station on the opposite side of the mayor] peaceably going through their employment under an asserted right by this railway company, their employers, and if any man interfere with them I will instantly commit him. You now know my fixed determination.'

The mayor's brave action and dramatic declaration brought a period of relative calm to the troubled scene, with the Hill & Moore men talking quietly among themselves and the S&B workmen just pottering about on their work site. Following up the initiative he had seized, His Worship formally read the Riot Act and ordered the crowd to disperse. Again he was successful, although the SVR men retired only as far as an adjoining field, where they were supplied with food and ale from a wagon.

At this stage the whole sorry affair might have petered out had not Baker, the SVR engineer, then arrived by train accompanied by Thomas Hill and Stephen Moore. They were soon engaged in a bitter altercation with the Shrewsbury & Birmingham officers, which was further fuelled when the S&B men began unloading cinders from wagon to barrow at the transhipment site. The time was just 2.15 pm when the contractors called upon the S&B to halt this work, maintaining that it was damaging the line for which they were responsible. Hill summoned reinforcements from the dinner crowd and was promptly placed in custody, the mayor himself making the arrest.

Quickly the police formed up on the embankment as the SVR reinforcements tried to rescue their leader. They were driven back, but not without a great deal of noise, threats and confusion. Again the mayor expostulated with the ringleaders and must have felt considerable relief when an engine and 30-40 empty wagons arrived from the station and the SVR men were ordered to climb in. With Moore and Lee on the footplate the train set off northwards, leaving the law and order party to congratulate themselves on the outcome.

But their feelings proved premature. Within a few minutes shouting could be heard from the direction taken by the train, and, dashing forward to investigate, the police found that it had gone only as far as Cannock Road bridge, where the S&B train had previously been stabled. The Stour Valley men had apparently disembarked there and overturned four wagons of the rival stock, and soon the two forces were again in violent collision, characterised by a lot of abuse and a great deal of stone-throwing. Again the Riot Act was read, then the police and soldiery waded into the fray, the former leading and with their cutlasses at the ready. Panic gripped the stone-throwers who were soon falling over one another to escape the steel blades bearing down on them. Most escaped serious injury, but one luckless fellow was badly cut on the back, and many more were arrested before order could be sufficiently restored to allow S&B staff to remove the obstruction and allow the 2.25 pm passenger train into the station.

Baker, realising that the situation was getting out of hand, now proposed an 'arrangement', and the principals met in the station waiting room to try to work something out. There they continued to argue, mainly because the mayor wanted to leave the original S&B men on their site and the SVR representatives wanted everyone withdrawn. Hill and Moore, the former apparently released to participate, argued that they were responsible for the track for 12 months after completion, and Hill threatened that he would again send his men in if anyone tampered with it. Fortunately, it was now nearly 5 o'clock, and justified the mayor in deciding that no more work could be done that day and that the site should thus be cleared completely.

After the rip-roaring affairs on site, the battle was now to be transferred to the courtroom, losing little of its ferocity in the process. First the LNWR/Stour Valley party approached the local magistrates on the Tuesday seeking to have Hill & Moore granted possession of the railway embankment from Cannock bridge to Canal Street bridge. However, when the mayor was sent for he would have none of this until the men arrested for breach of the peace had appeared on the Thursday. Meantime the S&B had gone to the Vice Chancellor for an injunction to maintain the status quo, and the legal scene began to show all the signs of maintaining the full tradition of the site confrontation, albeit with the insults much polished and the language and protocol duly legal. The conflict reached its climax on 20 July when Moore, Hill and Knowles, with others, appeared before the magistrates charged with unlawful and riotous assembly and with over-

turning four wagons, thereby endangering the safety of passengers.

The Shrewsbury & Birmingham had engaged Mr Serjeant Allen to appear for them, and he set out to earn his fee right from the opening address. This was comprehensive and vehement, painting the LNWR as avaricious and devious, daringly opposed by the valiant and struggling S&B whose interest was just to provide more rail communication for the public good. After flattering the mayor, who was on the bench, Allen went on:

'I say that right was not in the London and North Western. Messrs Moore and Hill were in the position of persons who had only an easement in the land; the land was in the possession of the proprietors of the Shrewsbury and Wolverhampton line, in conjunction with the proprietors of the Stour Valley; but it was de facto in possession of the Wolverhampton and Shrewsbury company. . . If a man contracts to repair my house, is he to come and eject me?'

Of the defendants he asked:

'Have they a right with arms and a numerous concourse to excite the fears of the peaceable inhabitants? Have they a right to obstruct the. . .line to the danger and injury of passengers?'

Mr Huddleston, for the defence, started off by complaining that having to wait while Col Hogg and others gave evidence had weakened his position in refuting Allen's references to the LNWR as 'the blackest-hearted villains that ever existed and dreadful wretches'. He then expressed himself not only willing, but anxious, to have his clients committed to the Assizes, but wanted to put the record straight on the background and commented that

'. . .it was quite obvious that the special retainer of my learned friend was to make a good speech abusing everybody who did not deserve it, and justifying some who did not want it, and that the real object of the "struggling company" [the S&B] was to give forth to the world the magnificent speech. . .teeming with torrents of abuse against the London and North Western. . .'

He went on to say that it was ludicrous to suggest that the LNWR was keeping the Stour Valley line closed to avoid competition when the reality was the S&B's efforts to have its line purchased; 'They won't buy us - abuse them until they do' was the order of the day, according to the LNWR/SVR counsel. On the purely legal issue, Huddleston maintained that Hill & Moore were under

contract to the SVR to keep the line in repair and anyone else was a trespasser, except for the purpose of running the trains. A telling point was the comment that the aggressors were clearly those provided with armbands - a prepared army - and that they might well find themselves in the dock instead.

All this rhetoric and abuse achieved very little, the defendants being bound over to appear at the next Assizes, the principals in surety of £500 each and the others of £50. The disputes over the wider issues were left to the warring railways much as before, and that peace was decidedly no nearer we shall see with some force in the next chapter.

A Regional Railways unit passes the site of the 1850 dispute at Wolverhampton.
One can picture the forces massed at each level ready for action!

7
WOLVERHAMPTON:
ROUND TWO

Following the dramatic events of the preceding chapter, the chairman of the Shrewsbury & Birmingham Railway tried to initiate a move towards peace between the three warring railways. He put forward conciliatory proposals to the LNWR, but these foundered on the unwillingness of the Shrewsbury & Chester to forfeit the right to reduce fares to compensate Liverpool passengers for the Mersey crossing. Unable to come to any arrangement with the London & North Western, which held the whip hand over access to Birmingham by its control of the Stour Valley project, the two Shrewsbury companies turned to the Great Western Railway instead. On 10 January 1851 these three entered into a traffic agreement for the interchange of goods and the division of the consequent receipts according to mileage. The GWR would soon be extending north from Banbury, and in the meantime the gap between the systems could be bridged by canal. To facilitate this the S&B constructed a branch to Victoria Basin to take over from the hard-won temporary exchange facility.

The Wolverhampton papers had a period of believing all might now be well on the railway scene, but at Euston there was no intention of taking the GWR intrusion lying down. At S&B meetings during the first half of 1851 the LNWR worked through its faction within the Shrewsbury & Birmingham camp to create mayhem in the company's affairs. Using its standard tactic of purchasing shares for nominees and tabling an attractive takeover offer, the LNWR party resisted

Protagonists:
Shrewsbury & Birmingham
Railway and London & North
Western Railway

Location:
South of Wolverhampton
High Level station

Date:
February-April and 1 December
1851 and subsequently

every attempt by the directors to secure approval for their deal with the GWR, which by now had expanded into provisional proposals for amalgamation in 1856 or 1857.

The problems started at the S&B half-yearly meeting called on 12 February to endorse the GWR agreement, and which instead appointed a Committee of Shareholders to examine the company's affairs. Directors Geach and Captain Probyn, and one of the auditors, roundly attacked the management, but got a sharp response from secretary Knox with some allegations of his own about Geach's dealings with the Oxford, Worcester & Wolverhampton Railway. At a resumed meeting on 12 March the uproar reached new heights, with the LNWR adherents raising questions about the traffic committee's activities, Knox's private involvement with the cinder traffic and the tactics used by canvassers calling on those shareholders who had

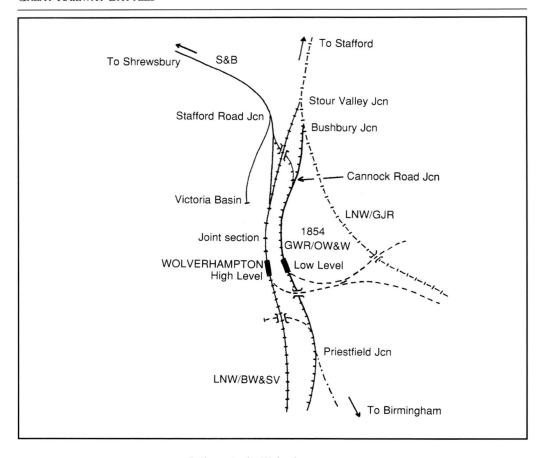

To Stafford

To Shrewsbury   S&B

Stour Valley Jcn

Stafford Road Jcn

Bushbury Jcn

Cannock Road Jcn

Victoria Basin

LNW/GJR

Joint section

1854
GWR/OW&W

WOLVERHAMPTON
High Level

Low Level

Priestfield Jcn

LNW/BW&SV

To Birmingham

Railways in the Wolverhampton area.

sent in proxies supporting the LNWR cause. The Committee dropped a bombshell by reporting a provisional agreement to transfer the S&B undertaking to the LNWR for a 3-4 per cent dividend, which was to be paid for out of the company's own earnings! Further uproar followed this announcement.

The second meeting was eventually adjourned to consider this unprecedented situation, and later in March the company issued a formal reply to the investigating committee, backed by counsel's opinion, and showing clearly the illegality, absurdity and financial folly of the so-called agreement with the LNWR. Yet a further meeting was on 4 April held to consider the matter and was to herald four days of argument, abuse and confusion.

The meeting on 4 April started off with queries about the election of directors and another attack on Knox. They were met with a pithy reminder that S&B traffic was up 30-40 per cent while that of the LNWR had actually gone down! A letter from the latter company was then produced and triggered off more outbursts, with the newspaper reporting:

'A cry was raised that some present were not shareholders and an attempt was made to weed out such individuals. One shareholder was observed approaching one of these supposed unlucky individuals with his stick raised, accompanied by sundry gesticulations, indicating that he must withdraw.'

By the third evening the chairman, W. Ormsby Gore, was reduced to quietly reading a copy of *Household Words*, then putting on a white nightcap and feigning sleep in an attempt to reduce the tension. However, despite this theatrical performance and the use of the LNWR's own trick of handing out shares to their own supporters, the directors lost the day. A resolution accepting the LNWR terms was carried and the triumphant splinter group went on to hold its own extension meeting, vote out the former directors, replace them, then ratify the agreement with the LNWR by using a replica of the Shrewsbury & Birmingham seal. During the course of these proceedings, on 7 May, Mr Geach maintained:

'All knew the disgraceful course. . .taken by the directors to resist the wishes of the shareholders. He would say advisedly that for the directors to come to a meeting and endeavour to get rid of the will of the majority by repeatedly moving adjournments, and by furnishing their officers with a few shares for the occasion, was the most disgraceful course he ever knew men to take.'

He was also rather upset by the fact that an attempt to capture the company's books by stealth had failed. The secretary had wisely moved them to safety.

The elected directors of the S&B followed the breakaway group's meeting with one of their own, which continued through the following day and on into the Friday. At this meeting the rebels made their protest, then walked out, after which the loyal shareholders confirmed the agreement with the Great Western Railway with the proper seal and revoked the powers of the Committee of Investigation. The occasion was marked by a long and lively speech from Mr Serjeant Allen yearning for some return on his investment. Modestly but cleverly, Knox countered this by using one of Allen's earlier utterances against him. The breakaway group had really achieved little except to put a propaganda tool into the hands of the LNWR, and that company, which still held all the cards by

controlling the Stour Valley line and its rate of construction, now turned its attentions to disrupting the Shrewsbury & Chester.

Around the middle of 1851 there were rumours that the LNWR was planning to run a train from Wellington to Wolverhampton in order to back up the spurious takeover agreement. The S&B marshalled a considerable force of platelayers and took out a section of rail to prevent this, but the precautions proved unnecessary and the emphasis moved towards the fact that the Stour Valley line was now completed but still lay unused despite every sort of pressure from the S&B and the Wolverhampton community. Out of patience at last, the former gave notice that it would apply to Parliament for powers to open the line itself, and thus provoked the LNWR into fixing an opening date. This was to be on 1 December.

On 25 November the Board of Trade approved the opening of the railway between Bushbury Junction, just north of Wolverhampton, and Birmingham Navigation Street. About the same time the S&B formally advised the LNWR of its plans to operate over the new line in furtherance of its running powers, and was told that these had been invalidated by the agreement with the GWR. As the S&B pointed out, the traffic arrangements with that company did not amount to amalgamation, and the 1847 agreement clearly indicated that only complete amalgamation could deprive it of the right to run to Birmingham.

Placards began to appear in Wolverhampton announcing the intention of the Shrewsbury & Birmingham Railway to operate trains from the new joint station to Birmingham from the day of opening, Monday 1 December 1851. The challenge caused consternation at Euston where senior officials discussed the matter on the preceding Saturday and instructed the secretary to take action. This he did late on the Saturday night with the resultant letter rushed north by train to Birmingham and delivered to the S&B secretary on the Sunday. At the same time copies were produced in placard form and exhibited in Wolverhampton and along the Stour Valley route, saying:

'The directors of the London and North Western Railway are compelled to announce the postponement for a time of the intended opening of this [Stour Valley] railway. The unavoidable necessity for this step will be explained by a reference to the annexed letter. The directors deeply regret the inconvenience which must result from the suspension, and they assure the public that not a moment will be lost in taking those steps which are best fitted to insure the safe and speedy opening of the line.

London and North Western
Railway Office
Birmingham, Sunday.'

'Euston-square, London, Saturday night

SIR - Having failed to obtain the concurrence of your directors in the proposal made to you in my letter of November 22, for the adoption of the necessary measures to decide the question at issue between the two companies, by an appeal to the Court, "at the most speed, and least expensive manner," or to obtain any assurance from your directors that they would abstain from acting upon their declared intention forcibly to use with their engines and carriages the Stour Valley railway on Monday next, in defiance of the protest of this company, it becomes the duty of the directors to consider what course they ought to pursue in the emergency caused by your proceedings.

Mature consideration of the imminent risk to the public from a hostile attempt such as that you have threatened, has led the directors to the conclusion not to incur the responsibility of opening the line under such circumstances. They are deeply sensible of the inconvenience and loss which the public, in common with their own proprietors, will sustain by the delay thus unavoidably caused; but this considera-

tion is outweighed by the apprehension for the public safety from your threatened proceedings.

Having waited in vain for the promised answer of your directors, through Mr Roy, the directors of this company have felt constrained to make a representation of the circumstances to the Railway Department of the Board of Trade, and to apprise them of the necessity which has arisen for postponing the opening of the line as the only means of avoiding the danger to be anticipated from a collision, and to afford an opportunity of adopting the necessary measures for insuring the public safety.

I am instructed to make this communication to you officially and

I am, your obedient servant,
CHARLES E. STEWART, Secretary

(To) J. F. Nicol Esq, Secretary to the Shrewsbury and Birmingham Railway, Wolverhampton.'

On the fateful Monday morning people began arriving at the new Wolverhampton station soon after eight o'clock. Somehow they sensed the excitement of a confrontation and the numbers continued to grow until several thousand would-be spectators were jostling for a good position. Among them were a few genuine passengers intent upon catching the first train, which was due to leave for Birmingham shortly after 9 o'clock. Well before its departure time a special arrived over the Stour Valley metals bringing LNWR officials and support staff, including a posse of railway policemen. The observant among those watching would have seen that an engine had also been brought up to block the other running line.

The stakes were raised when an official S&B placard announced that, notwithstanding what had been said about postponement, its trains would run to Birmingham over the Stour Valley route! At this, secretary Stewart and his LNWR colleagues, along with the S&B's Joseph Walker, set off to call upon the mayor in fear of a breach of the peace. That

A pre-Grouping view of the frontage of Wolverhampton High Level station. *Wolverhampton Library*

A present-day view of the London end of Wolverhampton station, looking south,
with down InterCity and up Regional Railways services, the latter in a similar position to the controversial
S&B train as it progressed towards the disputed Stour Valley line.

gentleman, mindful of the affair at the other end of the station the previous year, lost no time in summoning the Chief Constable and his men and asking the 50th Regiment of Foot for some of the soldiers it had stationed in the town.

Meanwhile, back at the railway station, a service from Shrewsbury had arrived at 9 o'clock carrying some passengers wishing to travel forward to Birmingham. After a lot of discussion among the S&B senior staff, the stock had been re-marshalled to form a short train consisting of the engine, a 3rd Class carriage and a brake-van. All this movement took place at the S&B end of the platform, but once completed the train, which was now loaded with S&B staff and workmen, began to draw forward, whistling defiantly as it progressed. A great cheer went up from the crowd as the challenging progression continued through the joint station towards the commencement of the Stour Valley metals, ignoring the detonators placed there and the red flags being waved by the LNWR party. Behind these, just beyond the up signal and bridge, was the LNWR locomotive *Swift* plus brake-van, no doubt using its whistle to signal suitable defiance. Baker, the SVR engineer, was on the footplate and was later alleged to have had rails taken up and a locomotive derailed to ensure the complete blockage of the line in the Birmingham direction.

Watched by the huge crowd of spectators and the combined police and soldiery, the S&B train tried to establish its right of passage. At a safe but purposeful speed it moved forward until contact was made with the buffers of *Swift*, which was given enough forward steam to ensure that it withstood the challenge. The Stour Valley driver, Newbold, was asked to clear the obstruction, but was told by Baker to do no such thing, and once more the cavalier actions of the two railways had brought them to a public impasse; 'a scene of great confusion and excitement', as the *Wolverhampton Chronicle & General Advertiser* called it.

Again the matter went straight to the Magistrates Court, where the contest was quite as keen if less physical. There was con-

siderable argument about what previous notices had been given, and a strong LNWR urging that the S&B locomotives had not been approved for passage over the Stour Valley line in accordance with the Railway Clauses Consolidation Act. To this the S&B replied that they were the same locomotives already operating over the joint S&B/Shropshire Union (LNWR) section between Shrewsbury and Wellington!

The S&B case was based on obstruction as defined in the General Regulation of Railways Act, viz 'That from and after the passing of this Act every person who shall wilfully do or cause anything to be done in such a manner as to obstruct any engine or carriage using any railway. . .shall be guilty of a misdemeanour'. Mr Peele, prosecuting engineer Baker and driver Newbold, maintained that the defence suggestion that there might be a collision was ludicrous, as there had never been one on the rest of the S&B's line. In its turn the LNWR maintained that the Stour Valley line was not open for traffic, but this, too, brought a riposte in the reminder that the LNWR party themselves arrived in Wolverhampton by train!

After all the argument and counter-argument the magistrates offered a masterly summing up, but concluded that they were really not empowered to commit Baker and Newbold for trial. They urged the parties towards a peaceful solution and to avoid committing a breach of the peace. Mr Carter, for the LNWR, maintained that his clients had already given strict instructions that the resistance of their staff was to be passive, but felt obliged to ask 'his friend on the other side, Mr William Roy, to withdraw the threat which he had made'. Mr Roy, clearly no lover of the LNWR, had apparently remarked at one stage of the morning's events: 'If you do not remove your engine we will remove it for you'.

A final shot came from the S&B's Mr Peele, who offered a period of restraint if the LNWR would put the whole issue before the Court of Chancery, but reminded the magistrates that the case of the LNWR fares via Stafford had been before that body since 1849 with no judgement yet available. The

8
THE 'ALARMING RIOT'
AT MICKLETON

The railway from Worcester to Oxford follows a level course through the fertile Vale of Evesham, then climbs for over 4 miles at 1 in 100 to surmount the Cotswold ridge before heading on south-east through a landscape of pretty woods, winding rivers and mellow stone buildings. This green and pleasant countryside seems an unlikely setting for a scene of mass human confrontation that required the presence of magistrates, constabulary and soldiers to control; and yet this is just what happened back in the middle of 1851, at a spot near the normally peaceful village of Mickleton.

The climb up Campden Bank starts in earnest after Honeybourne station and rises steadily by means of cuttings and embankments, past the site of the 1937 Mickleton Halt - a nightmare for train drivers having to restart in slippery conditions - to the cutting that precedes the 887-yard Campden Tunnel. Leaving the tunnel via a second cutting, the route passes over Battle Crossing and through the site of the former Campden station, which served the pleasant Cotswold woollen centre of Chipping Campden. The contract for building the 4-mile section of line that included the tunnel was the one that prompted the so-called Battle of Mickleton, and it may be that Battle Crossing, still functioning as a modern barrier-crossing, is aptly named.

The line was built originally by the Oxford, Worcester & Wolverhampton Railway, a scheme that started auspiciously enough as a line to meet the demands of

Protagonists:
Oxford, Worcester & Wolverhampton Railway and its contractors, Peto & Betts, versus displaced contractors Williams & Marchant

Location:
Campden Tunnel, east of Honeybourne

Date:
10-21 July 1851

West Midlands manufacturers for a new route to London. Supported with financial guarantees by the Great Western Railway, all the omens for the new railway seemed good. But then relations between offspring and parent became strained as the problems of construction and finance mounted, until acrimony abounded and the company's troubles multiplied on every side. Before the OW&W eventually returned to the GWR camp it was to seek its own extension to London and to exchange passengers with the Great Western's bitter rival, the LNWR. Amid this wider conflict the affair at Mickleton did not seem wholly out of place.

The original construction contract for Campden Tunnel and its approaches was held for a short period by Gale & Warden, but in February 1847 it passed to Messrs Williams, Aykroyd & Price. Despite other

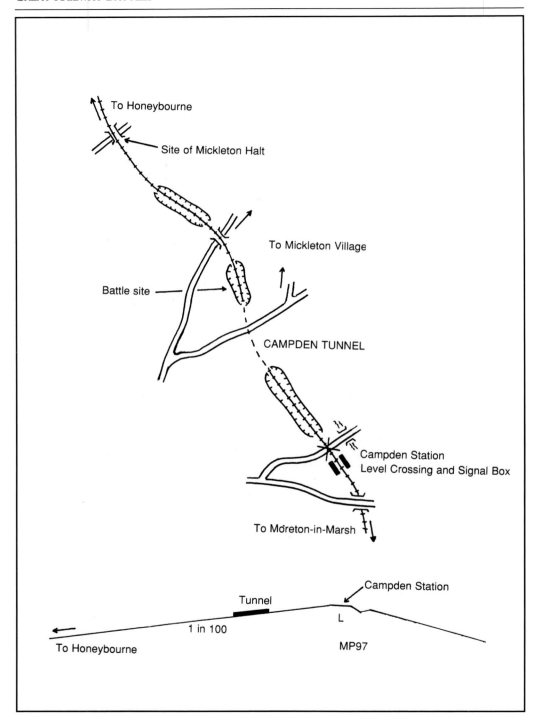

The area around Campden Tunnel.

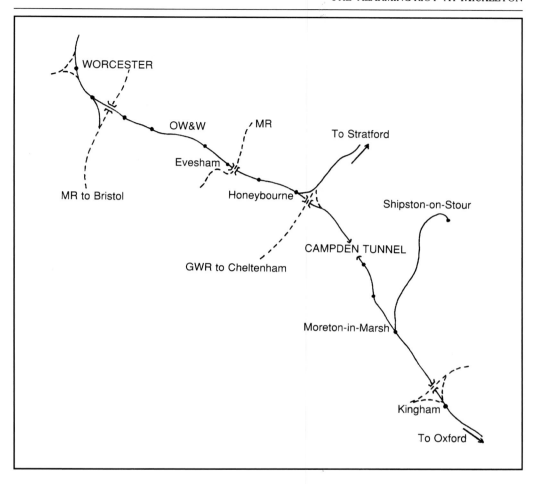

The route of the Oxford, Worcester & Wolverhampton Railway over the Cotswolds.

contracts in the North West, this firm seemed lacking in both adequate funds and effective organisation. They soon showed themselves poor contenders to meet the challenges of the Cotswold oolitic limestone and the drainage problems arising from the 1 in 100 gradient, drawing down criticism upon themselves from Brunel in his capacity as the line's engineer, and falling into dispute between one another. By the end of 1848 work on the tunnel section was seriously in arrears.

In 1849 Aykroyd and Price withdrew from the partnership and Williams became associated with a new partner, R. M. Marchant, who was related to Brunel and who had been

acting as one of his assistant engineers on the Campden section. Brunel did warn Marchant of the gamble he was taking by throwing in his lot with the notoriously unpredictable business of railway construction, and the young man's dreams of fame and fortune must have seemed considerably less substantial when the OW&W was forced to suspend all construction work in June 1849 owing to mounting financial problems.

This period was a bad one for railways generally and, indeed, for the nation as a whole. The years 1845-47 were marked by the failure of potato crops, poor corn harvests and inflated prices for imported cotton. With so many railway schemes afoot, capital was already hard to come by, and when Europe was swept by revolution in 1848 and 1849 those few who had cash available lacked the confidence to part with it. The GWR, with troubles of its own, declined the OW&W invitation to finish the line or to contribute to the further £1.5 million estimated as the cost of completion. The whole situation appeared exceedingly gloomy, not least because contractors like Williams & Marchant were suing for caretaking and compensation costs.

Matters began to improve in 1850. The American market recovered, which helped exports and made Britain's money position easier. In turn, the OW&W benefited by a better response to its offer of £850,000 in preference shares authorised under a new Act, and felt strong enough to reject its understandings with the Great Western and remove the Paddington directors from the board. One of the new investors responding to the offer of preference shares was Sir Morton Peto, of the railway contracting firm Peto & Betts, who, through his nominee on the OW&W board, was soon to make his presence felt. Not surprisingly, negotiations were quickly put in hand for Peto to take over work on the Cotswold section of the line and, as part of the same process, the Mickleton tunnel contractors, Williams & Marchant, were given a deadline for the completion of their portion. This warning, which was given at the end of 1850, appears to have had little effect, for by June 1851 they were being told to increase the workforce in order to get more done or to quit the works altogether.

Matters came to a head in the following month, and although reports of the events differ considerably, it is clear that a serious confrontation erupted between the OW&W and its contractor. The process began when the company's agent, no doubt under instruction, put in a sub-contractor to help with the Marchant section. When the latter's men refused to co-operate, doubtless seeing this as a step towards their own replacement, tempers rose to the point where Marchant's agent felt obliged to warn the Chipping Campden magistrates that there was trouble

in the offing. According to George Steen, who was acting for Marchant, the sub-contractor, George Cole, was threatening to remove the Williams & Marchant men and their tools by force and to take over the tunnel works that were causing so much anxiety.

The law officers reacted swiftly, swearing in special constables and asking for help from the Chief Constable in Cheltenham. With their forces duly marshalled, two magistrates visited the tunnel site on the following day, Friday 11 July, to find there a body of men from each of the opposing camps busy waving pick-axes and shovels and hurling abuse at one another. Beer was in plentiful supply and its consumption helped to swell the noise and confusion. By this time Brunel himself was on the scene and was all for completing the process Cole had started. However, in response to urgings from the magistrates, Brunel made one more effort to reach a satisfactory agreement with his former assistant. The magistrates themselves, clearly uneasy about the chances of the negotiations succeeding, took the opportunity to summon reinforcements!

An evening of discussion, frequently noisy and abusive, came to nought and the participants eventually retired to their beds with nothing resolved. After snatching a few hours sleep, Brunel returned early the following morning, hoping to steal a march on his adversaries. But Marchant was not to be caught napping that easily, and soon armed and angry men from the two sides were again facing one another across the site. Tempers were now so inflamed that the magistrates read the Riot Act and ordered their forces, substantially reinforced since the previous day, and armed with cutlasses, to start disarming the vociferous and threatening navvies. Brunel himself was angry by this time, but decided to avoid making the situation worse and called off his 'troops' to allow a further uneasy peace to return to the works.

But nothing had been resolved. The Marchant incumbents posted 'sentries' to protect their occupation of the site and the rival forces continued to look for ways of taking possession. This bizarre situation, turning sleepy woodland and a normally near empty countryside into a scene of restless menace, continued throughout the next week. While officers of the railway and its contractors conferred, a large number of unemployed navvies roamed the quiet country lanes around the tunnel, increasing the tension on the site itself and the apprehensions of those who lived nearby.

The stand-off had to end, and Brunel, not noted for either patience or half-hearted action, resolved to mount a surprise take-over with overwhelming numbers. At the end of the second week following the initial 'battle', arrangements were made to bring in large contingents of workmen from adjoining Peto & Betts contracts, these making their way in waggons, in omnibuses and on foot from places as far away as Fenny Compton, until a force estimated variously between 500 and 2,000 men had been assembled by the evening of Sunday 20 July. The intention

was to use the classic tactic of a dawn attack and take over the site by sheer weight of numbers before the Marchant men had got themselves organised for the normal Monday resumption of work.

The arrival of so many working men in the remote rural area around Mickleton did not escape the notice of the local inhabitants, by now well aware of what was going on and getting increasingly nervous as the conflict escalated. Word was hurriedly sent to the magistrates and by 2 am a Justice of the Peace from Bretforton had joined the crowd on the site, supported by a force of constables and soldiers. All the ingredients of conflagration were present, a simmering unresolved dispute, hordes of men armed with the tools of their rough trade, a desperate railway needing to open its line and earn some money, and leaders under considerable pressures of their own. *The Times* provided a lurid account of what followed:

Today only a single line leads from the aptly named Battle Crossing through the now quiet countryside to the eastern portal of Campden Tunnel.

Looking towards Campden Tunnel from the west, this is the route that the attacking force
would have taken in the early hours of 21 July 1851, reaching the line from the modest country road up from
Mickleton village that runs beneath the bridge.

'On reaching the Worcester end of the tunnel Mr Cowdery with his gang of 200 men from Evesham and Wyre was met by Mr Marchant who dared anyone of Messrs Peto and Betts men to pass the bridge on pain of being shot, Mr Marchant himself being well supplied with pistols. Mr Cowdery, exercising great forbearance at the unseemly conduct of Mr Marchant, told his men on no account whatsoever to strike a blow. Mr Cowdery, finding that all expostulation was useless and Mr Brunel giving peremptory orders for Messrs Peto and Betts men to proceed and take everything in the line, a rush was made to the men which after a few seconds was repelled with great force by Marchant and his men, the consequence was that several heads were broken and three men had their shoulders dislocated. Up to this time the navvies had not called in to req-

uisition the picks or pick-axes or shovels, but a man in the employ of Marchant having drawn pistols he was seized upon and his skull nearly severed in two.

This occurrence for a time daunted Marchant, and he left Messrs Peto and Betts men for an hour in undisputed possession on the ground. At the expiration of that time he returned with some three dozen policemen from the Gloucester Constabulary and some privates of the Gloucester Artillery accompanied by two magistrates of the place, who immediately commenced reading the Riot Act. At this juncture a melee had taken place on a high embankment and here several broken limbs had been a result of the conflict. About 2 o'clock Mr Charles Watson of Warwick arrived with upwards of 200 men, and the Great Western company who sent a similar number in order to assist them.

Marchant, now finding that all attempts at resistance were useless, from the vast majority in numbers of his opponents, gave in, and he and Mr Brunel adjourned, in order to come to an acceptable arrangement. In their absence a small batch of navvies again met and one of them had his little finger bitten off, another his head severely wounded. Eventually it was arranged that Messrs Cubitt and Stephenson were to be arbitrators and that the works were to be suspended for a fortnight.'

There appear to be several inaccuracies in *The Times*'s account. The most reliable versions put the conflict as taking place between 2 am and 8.30 am in the morning, but others record it as lasting well into the afternoon. The newspaper accounts had a lurid element and the official reports a defensive one, but whatever the exact truth, there is no doubt that the deep cutting used by the line between the modest road up from Mickleton village and the tunnel was the scene of a noisy and bitter confrontation from which Peto & Betts were able to gain control of the tunnel works. The defeated Marchant was brought near to ruin and found himself in the bankruptcy court within a few weeks. Brunel's warnings had proved disastrously right.

Campden Tunnel was eventually completed in the spring of 1852, the year in which the first portion of the OW&W - between Stourbridge and Evesham - was opened on 1 May. By this time Brunel had resigned his post as engineer and a Peto nominee was dominating the OW&W board, negotiating with Euston and trying hard to avoid the original requirement to lay broad gauge on the main line. At the Board of Trade Inspector's insistence, the company did agree to lay a third rail to create a mixed gauge track, and was then allowed to open the Evesham-Wolvercot Junction (Oxford) section on 4 June 1853. However, by 1854 traffic was being routed to Euston via Handborough and the Yarnton Loop and the GWR influence was at its lowest.

From 1856 the GWR faction on the OW&W board grew stronger and five years later was able to defeat a scheme for the railway to build its own independent access to London. Instead, the Old Worse & Worse, as the railway came to be known, opted for a working agreement with its broad gauge neighbour. As a constituent of the West Midland Railway and with Worcester joined to Hereford and thence to Abergavenny, the OW&W line and its branches was finally amalgamated with the GWR from 1 August 1863. The West Midland Railway added 267 miles to the latter's system, but brought the first narrow gauge trains to Paddington and sounded the death knell for the broad gauge.

The scene at Mickleton has now returned to one of pastoral serenity, and it is difficult to believe that so much violence was once exhibited there. The scars of the earthworks above the tunnel have been healed by many years' growth of trees and lesser vegetation, and the B4081 from Chipping Camden to Mickleton village looks just too quiet to have ever been the route of boisterous navvies bent on climbing up to the line beneath which it passes, and on to some grim fighting when they got there.

9
CONFRONTATION AT CLIFTON JUNCTION

In the early years of the railway system two companies struggled for supremacy in the traffic-rich territory to the north-west of Manchester. In a period of 15 years before they finally decided that amalgamation had more to offer than competition, the two veered back and forth between co-operation and confrontation, twice reaching the point of physical conflict and always keenly watchful of each other's every move and action.

One of the protagonists in this conflict was the East Lancashire Railway, a small and lively concern with its headquarters at Bolton Street station, Bury. It grew rapidly under strong leadership, and cherished ambitions to link its Bury-based system with trunk routes planned to the North East and to Scotland. Although these plans failed to fructify, the ELR's routes from Manchester to Accrington and then east to Colne and west to Preston and Liverpool were of sufficient strategic and traffic importance to bring the system into resounding conflict with its neighbour, the Lancashire & Yorkshire Railway.

The Lancashire & Yorkshire concern had started life as the Manchester & Leeds Railway, intended to emulate the success of the pioneer Liverpool & Manchester scheme and opening its main line eastwards to Normanton on 1 March 1841. This gave the company connections to York, Hull, Derby and Leicester, and ensured its future importance in the national system. The M&L subsequently joined with six other companies, including the Manchester, Bolton & Bury

| Protagonists: |
| East Lancashire Railway |
| and |
| Lancashire & Yorkshire Railway |
| Location: |
| Clifton Junction, |
| between Salford and Bolton |
| Date: |
| 12 March 1849 and subsequently |

Railway and the Liverpool & Bury Railway, to become the Lancashire & Yorkshire Railway in 1847, with the system eventually growing to one of just over 600 route miles. In this form it was to become one of the major constituents of the London Midland & Scottish Railway under the Grouping arrangements of 1923.

Manchester business interests were behind both the East Lancashire and Lancashire & Yorkshire concerns. One such group conceived and promoted the Manchester, Bury & Rossendale Railway, which came into being in October 1843 with the express object of linking Manchester with the mill towns to the north. It secured Parliamentary approval on 4 July 1844 and gave its contractors, Messrs Pauling & Henfrey, the green light to make a start on the £300,000 works, which had already been discussed and agreed.

The same group also promoted the Blackburn, Burnley, Accrington & Colne

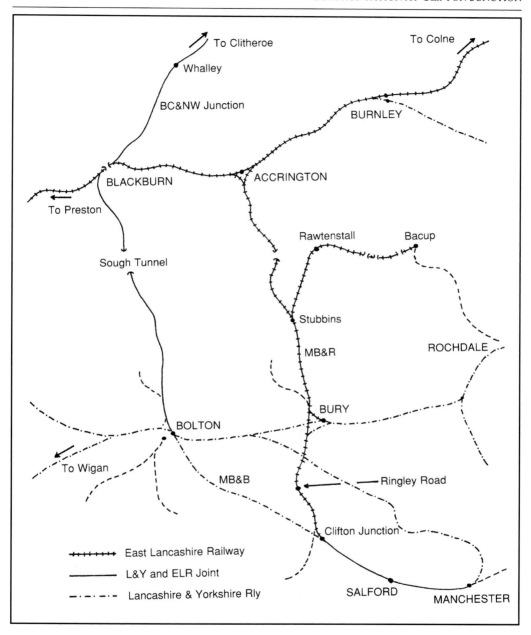

The East Lancashire Railway and neighbouring lines.

Extension Railway, which was to take the MB&R line north from Stubbins Junction to Accrington, then west to meet the Blackburn & Preston Railway and east to meet the Leeds & Bradford Railway at Colne. On 25 November 1844 the two groups agreed to merge as the East Lancashire Railway, obtaining Parliamentary approval for this in an Act of 21 July 1845. Under this new title the BBA&CE scheme was ratified on 30 June

1845 with a capital of £530,000 and powers to sell to the MB&R proprietors. The July Act also endorsed the inclusion of the Blackburn & Preston Railway and of the Liverpool, Ormskirk & Preston in the new East Lancashire grouping. A sizeable and formidable railway was emerging.

Work on all these schemes proceeded quite quickly despite some tough gradients, difficult tunnels and a lot of awkward river crossings, with the line from Blackburn to Preston opening on 1 June 1846 and the Bury line on 25 September 1846 (public services from 28 September). The latter started at Clifton Junction on the MB&B's Manchester to Bolton route and followed the Irwell Valley north through Radcliffe to Bury, continuing as a double track to Stubbins, then becoming single for the section on to Rawtenstall. An extension to Newchurch was subsequently opened on 27 March 1848, and another $2\frac{1}{2}$ miles to Bacup added four years later.

The Extension Railway, for which the first contract was let on 13 October 1845, was to leave the Rawtenstall line at Stubbins, just north of Ramsbottom, and climb steeply through Helmshore to a summit at Baxenden before dropping even more steeply down to Accrington. From there fairly level branches would run west to join the Preston-Blackburn line at the latter point and east through Burnley to Colne to join the line from Todmorden at Burnley and the Leeds & Bradford Extension Railway at Colne.

A host of construction difficulties on the Stubbins-Accrington section were eventually overcome to permit opening on 17 August 1848. Accrington-Blackburn had been opened two months earlier and trains immediately started running through to Preston, with Burnley being added to the ELR system on 18 September of the same year, and Colne being reached on 1 February 1849. To the west, ELR services began running to and from Liverpool on 8 November 1849 to give the company a substantial and well-used network of railways.

Clause 252 of the original Manchester, Bury & Rawtenstall Railway Act had dealt with the movement of ELR trains forward from Clifton Junction, the running powers applying over the MB&B metals as far as Salford, then over the L&M into the Liverpool Road terminus at Manchester. By Clause 254 it provided for the intruding company to furnish details of its use of these powers 'to the clerk of the company of proprietor's or to their collector of tolls at the place where he attends for the collection of tolls'. Initially there seem to have been no problems, the Bury company sharing the cost of having a toll collector at Clifton station and handing to him the tickets collected from the passengers of up (Manchester-bound) trains, to be used as the basis for assessing the tolls due. Down trains presented no difficulty as the owning company was able to check the numbers boarding at its stations. Subsequently, to avoid all ELR trains having to stop at Clifton, which was then quite a remote spot, the practice changed to one under which the ELR provided returns of the numbers upon which tolls were due and duly remitted to the MB&B company on that basis.

The year 1847 saw the beginning of a heightening of tension between the local railways. The ELR was growing rapidly, but was dramatically overtaken in size when the L&Y was formed. East Lancashire interests opposed the inclusion of the Manchester, Bolton & Bury Railway in the new group - doubtless concerned about its dependence upon that concern for the final entry into Manchester - and became even more anxious in 1848 when the newly formed L&Y empire intruded into the ELR heartland at Bury by an extension from the 1841 branch at Heywood. Nor was the L&Y very happy with the situation, for completion of the ELR routes to Liverpool and Colne would soon create a new challenge for the extensive and lucrative traffic moving between Lancashire and Yorkshire.

It was against this background that the L&Y, as successors to the Manchester, Bolton & Bury Railway, advised the East Lancashire Railway that it wished to revert to the former practice of having all up ELR trains stop at Clifton to surrender tickets to L&Y staff. The smaller company refused,

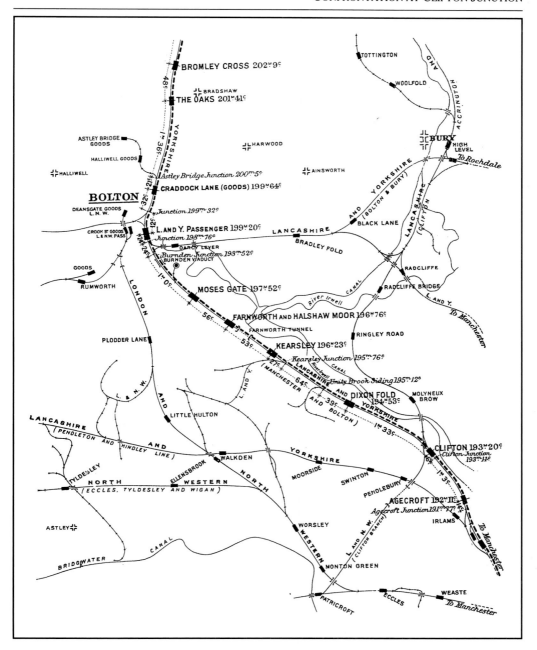

The Clifton Junction-Bury-Bolton lines, as shown in the Midland Railway Distance Diagrams.

believing the action to be a piece of spite 'made for the sake of annoyance and detention, since the two companies have become competitors for the traffic between Bradford and Manchester.' The L&Y then notified the ELR at the beginning of March 1849 that from Monday the 12th it would 'take measures for preventing the East Lancashire trains for Manchester coming upon the Lancashire and Yorkshire line, until the passengers' tickets were given up to the officers of the Lancashire and Yorkshire Railway.' This was fighting talk, containing no hint of compromise and brooking no negotiation, and there was no way in which the ELR could or would take such an ultimatum lying down. The battle lines had been drawn.

The Bolton-Salford line followed the north-west/south-east course of its canal predecessor, approaching the junction at Clifton with a long, straight section raised well above the surrounding countryside. From the north the East Lancashire's line took a long curve after Radcliffe to follow the valley contour through Ringley Road and approach the Bolton line on a converging south-east course, joining it shortly after the 13-arch viaduct over the Irwell. The elevation of the two routes made them an ideal stage for the events of Monday 12 March 1849, and an audience duly appeared, alerted in the mysterious way in which news of potentially dramatic events does seem to spread around.

On the battlefield itself no action was taken against the early morning stopping trains to Manchester. They followed their usual course and procedures, regulated by the signal cabin in the vee of the junction and carrying the passengers of both the rival railways and those of the Blackburn, Darwen & Bolton Railway, whose trains joined the route at the latter point. However, senior officers and other staff of both the East Lancashire and Lancashire & Yorkshire companies began to arrive at around 10 o'clock, and soon the latter had a formidable array of top brass on the spot; Captain Laws, the L&Y managing director, was accompanied by traffic superintendent Blackmore, goods superintendent Hinmers and locomotive superintendent Hurst, each with his own entourage and with sufficient artisans and labourers to carry the blockade plans into action.

The L&Y company had made extensive preparations to implement its threat to deny ELR trains access to the Salford line until tickets had been given up. Extra signalmen had been positioned along the line to make

sure that traffic disruptions did not affect safety, and a train of empty coaching stock had been moved into the area to carry passengers forward to Manchester if the blockade had to be put into effect. The fact that this train could also be used as part of the blockading process was not overlooked. The police had also been alerted, and detachments from the Bury and Pendleton forces had, at the invitation of the ELR, taken up a position inside the ELR signal cabin, from which they would have a vantage point to keep an eye on the proceedings.

The first ELR non-stop service was due at about 10.30. Before it arrived the L&Y 'heavies' swung into action, taking a balk of timber that had been brought to the scene previously and placing it across the tracks just beyond the junction points. To hold the heavy beam in place crowbars were hammered into the trackbed over and behind the obstruction. The train of six empty coaches was then backed up to the junction, coming to a stand on the up line just beyond the points and with its engine at the Manchester end, as can be seen in the engraving on page 80.

When the train from Bury arrived it was brought to a halt at the junction, and the L&Y collectors went forward to collect tickets. They were out of luck, however, for all the passengers had surrendered theirs to the ELR staff at Ringley Road as they had been doing for some time previously. The tensions were now heightening and each of the protagonists seemed quite intent on having their way. The obstruction had been intended to enforce the L&Y's decision to collect tickets, but with these items $2^{1}/_{2}$ miles away at Ringley Road, the L&Y management found itself in something of a quandary. Its objective could no longer be achieved, but to remove the obstruction would be to sacrifice the whole point of the exercise and would represent a massive climb-down.

As it turned out, the decision was taken out of the L&Y's hands. Although the demeanour of everyone on site had so far remained very cool and proper, the ELR was not content to leave the initiative with its opponents. ELR men were sent to hammer the crowbars loose and lift away the timber

In this view of what is now plain Clifton, looking towards Manchester, the former ELR route converged with the L&Y line at a point almost opposite the Class '150' three-car unit. Today the station enjoys a peak-hour service only.

On the east side of the line, the old cobbled approach road remains that once gave access to the East Lancashire Railway signal box in the vee of the junction.

balk. The driver of the Bury train was instructed to try to force his passage through and propel the blockading empty stock train before him. Nothing loth, he promptly opened the regulator of his engine and moved on to the rear of the 'enemy' coaches. The stakes were being raised, and the conflict was getting quite serious.

Seeing their opponents intent upon force, the L&Y officials made their counter-move. A down express was brought to a standstill and its engine commandeered, the driver being told to shunt over to the up line and reinforce the train already standing there. Five-foot driving wheels spun wildly as steam was fed into the 15 x 18-inch cylinders, but the ELR train could make no headway against heavier opposition and some thought, at least, would soon need to be given to the passengers who were peering out of the train windows or standing beside the track and either enjoying the contest or complaining vociferously.

Had it so wished, the L&Y could have continued to operate over the down line by removing the engineless express, but to even matters out the ELR then decided to block that by bringing forward a trainload of stone (which it just happened to have handy!) and pushing it foul of the junction points. Now no one could move, and soon other trains were drawn up beyond the obstruction until a total of eight were waiting, stretching for half a mile and full of angry passengers. One party threatened to send to Pendleton and hire a post-chaise, for which they vowed the offending railways would have to pay.

Things could not remain in this stalemate. Captain Laws made the first move by deciding to leave matters in the hands of his traffic superintendent and retiring from the scene. The latter, seeing the approach of noon with no apparent hope of resolving the issue, in turn decided to unravel the mess by removing the engine and empty train from the up line. The ELR followed suit and drew back its own obstruction so that traffic could, at last, begin to flow freely again. The original ELR train that had been the first subject of the blockade then went on its journey, sounding 'crows' on its whistle to celebrate the climbdown by the Lancashire & Yorkshire side.

Clearly, though, matters could not be left like that, and the *Illustrated London News*

reported on 24 March 1849 that Mr Hackin of the ELR and Captain Laws of the L&Y company met 'and came to an amicable arrangement'. The *Carlisle Patriot* of 31 March was a little more revealing and disclosed that the settlement discussion also embraced a dispute over the use of the hoist at the goods yard at Irwell Street, Salford. Of the main bone of contention, the newspaper records that 'arrangements have been entered into by which the East Lancashire Company secure to the Lancashire & Yorkshire full particulars in reference to the traffic from all parts of their line passing along the 4½ miles of railway belonging to the latter company and that in the form desired by the Lancashire & Yorkshire Company'.

This compromise patched up the difficulty over Clifton Junction, avoiding the need for ELR expresses to stop there but giving the

RAILWAY BLOCKADE AT CLIFTON STATION, NEAR MANCHESTER.

*The **Illustrated London News**'s view of the events at Clifton Junction.*

L&Y better figures than it had previously received and in a form dictated by that company. However, as the next chapter will reveal, more open conflict between the ELR and L&Y companies was still to come. Access to Manchester again became one of the bones of contention, with the ELR quarrelling with the London & North Western Railway over the use of the Salford-Victoria section and having to terminate its trains at Salford from February 1849.

By 1852 working relationships over the ELR's use of the line forward from Clifton Junction were becoming so bad that something just had to be done. At a meeting on 20 June of the following year the smaller concern decided to promote its own Bill for independent access to Manchester. Faced with this threat the L&Y saw the wisdom of making final peace over the Clifton Junction problem and agreed that the line between Clifton and Salford should become joint property, an arrangement that was carried into effect on 3 July 1854 with the passing of the Clifton & Manchester Railway Act.

Little remains at Clifton Junction today to mark the excitement of the events of 12 March 1849. Indeed, the East Lancashire company's main line to Accrington has been closed since 5 December 1966 and the surviving station on the former MB&B/L&Y line has only a limited peak-hour service. Clifton, no longer a junction, is just a modest affair of up and down platforms and simple shelters reached from the Bolton-end overbridge, and with the eastern end of its platforms weed-strewn and out of use.

A little way north, towards Clifton proper, an approach road to a small industrial area cuts through the former ELR line embankment. Beyond this, on the Bury side, the great stone viaduct over the Irwell is still standing and is visible from trains approaching Clifton from the Bolton direction. The station side of the embankment continues its overgrown course to the site of the former junction, at the end of the surviving up platform. The latter still has its cobbled approach road, which helps to create the right atmosphere for conjuring up the memory of the old ELR signal box that once stood just ahead, and of the day when police watched anxiously from its windows as two rival railways thoroughly disturbed the peace.

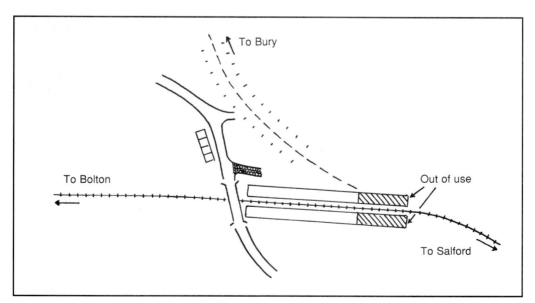

Clifton Junction station area in 1993.

10
THE REVENGE OF THE EAST LANCASHIRE RAILWAY

'**I**t is not at all astonishing that railway property should be so depreciated in value in comparison with other investments of this country when we have so constantly exposed to you glaring instances of the reckless and careless manner in which the affairs of different companies are conducted. We have been obliged, under a sense of strict duty, most reluctantly to allude to this subject in the case of the turnout of the East Lancashire engine drivers and we are sorry that we should, in so short an interval, [again] be obliged to call the attention of the public and the shareholders to the conduct of the same company.'

So thundered the *Blackburn Standard* under the heading 'Railway Blockade' in its issue of Wednesday 26 June 1850. It went on to provide lurid details of an incident that had taken place near Blackburn station four days earlier when the interests of the East Lancashire and Lancashire & Yorkshire Railways had once again come into head-on and uncompromising conflict. Curiously, few commentators relate this incident at Blackburn to the one at Clifton Junction the previous year, but the latter must still have rankled in the minds of the ELR management and there are some striking similarities in the tactics that were used. At Clifton Junction the L&Y had physically blocked ELR access to its line and imposed conditions for returning the situation to normal; at Blackburn the boot was on exactly the other foot!

> **Protagonists:**
> East Lancashire Railway and Bolton, Blackburn, Clitheroe & West Yorkshire Railway
>
> **Location:**
> Daisy Field Junction, Blackburn
>
> **Date:**
> 12-22 June 1850 and subsequently

The interests of the East Lancashire Railway and those of the Lancashire & Yorkshire concern had increasingly been coming into conflict, not only in terms of local traffic but also in the case of their wider ambitions. In the latter sphere the East Lancashire had on 1 February 1849 extended to Colne to meet the Leeds & Bradford Extension Railway and thus gain access to Yorkshire and its traffic. Later in that same year, but after the Clifton Junction incident, ELR trains also reached Liverpool, and the company laid on expresses to cater for the business between Yorkshire and the Mersey. Much to its chagrin and quite probably due to the L&Y's influence with the Midland, these were not allowed to run through to Bradford, and passengers were subjected to the inconvenience of a change at Colne.

This supposition of collusion to thwart the ELR's ambitions is supported by the fact that the Lancashire & Yorkshire also had a strong interest in routes from Manchester north-wards to Yorkshire. Within that territory, which the ELR would have liked to make its own, this interest centred on two smaller companies, viz the Blackburn, Darwen & Bolton Railway and the Blackburn, Clitheroe and North Western Junction Railway.

The BD&B concern originated in 1844, holding its first meeting on 27 September to consider John Watson's survey and subse-quently raising its planned capital to £300,000 because of the difficult terrain the line had to cross. Within a very short time the company was showing signs of ambition, deciding to add a line from Blackburn to Clitheroe to the Bolton-Blackburn line already decided upon. Its stated intention was to link up with the North Western Railway and thus, with the co-operation of the Manchester & Bolton company, create a trunk route from Manchester northwards.

The BD&B project obtained its Act on 30 June 1845, with a modification on 3 August, and by 13 September had awarded the con-struction contract. On 27 September the chairman cut the first sod at Darwen. Terence Flanagan, formerly with the Blackburn & Preston Railway, became the BD&B engineer in 1846 and fulfilled the same function for the Blackburn, Clitheroe & North Western Junction Railway which obtained its Act on 27 July 1846.

The BC&NW Bill provided for a line from Daisy Field, Blackburn, to a junction with the proposed North Western Railway at Long Preston. The most important branch was to the Leeds & Bradford Extension Railway at Elslack, and there was provision for a separate route through Blackburn to link up with the BD&B line south to Bolton. Opposed by the East Lancashire interests, this latter aspect passed the Commons but was rejected by the House of Lords, which provided for trains to use the ELR metals as the connection between the Bolton and Clitheroe lines. In the Blackburn, Clitheroe & North Western Junction Railway Act passed on 27 July 1846, sections 21 and 22 provided for the conditions of such use to be determined by arbitrators, one from each company, with a Board of Trade umpire in

the event of a dispute. Section 39 contained powers to sell the railway to the Blackburn, Darwen & Bolton concern.

In March 1847 the Bolton-Blackburn and Blackburn-Clitheroe projects decided to amalgamate, a development that was ratified by the Bolton, Blackburn, Clitheroe and West Yorkshire Railway Act of 9 July 1847. This title proved so cumbersome that the new company was usually known as the Blackburn Railway, this simplification being confirmed in a further Act in 1851. With its potential to reach both Bradford and Lancaster, it is not surprising that the BBC&WY was courted by both the East Lancashire Railway and the L&Y.

The East Lancashire Railway had already lost one round of the contest in that its pre-decessor's scheme for reaching Long Preston, the Clitheroe Junction Railway, had been rejected by Parliament in 1846 in favour of the BC&NW project. However, it had gained the big advantage of compelling its successful rival to pass through Blackburn via the ELR station and metals. This was to prove the root cause of the confrontation that took place in the middle of 1850, and which so offended the *Blackburn Standard*.

The BBC&WY line from Blackburn to Sough was opened on 3 August 1847, but the day was somewhat marred by the collapse of four arches of Tonge Viaduct on the section nearest Bolton. However, passengers flocked to the new railway and provided useful rev-enue for the completion of the route south-wards. By 6 June 1848 it was possible to run a short, experimental train over the whole route and six days later a single line was opened for traffic. The company managed to derail its first train on that day!

Not to be outdone in the rush to increase local service permutations, the East Lancashire Railway started operating between Blackburn and Accrington on 19 June 1848 and completed the Accrington-Stubbins Junction section on 17 August, to give Blackburn a second route to Manchester. Unhappily for the ELR, that of the Blackburn company was the shorter by 4 miles, and its trains were anything from 5 to 13 minutes quicker. The ELR looked likely

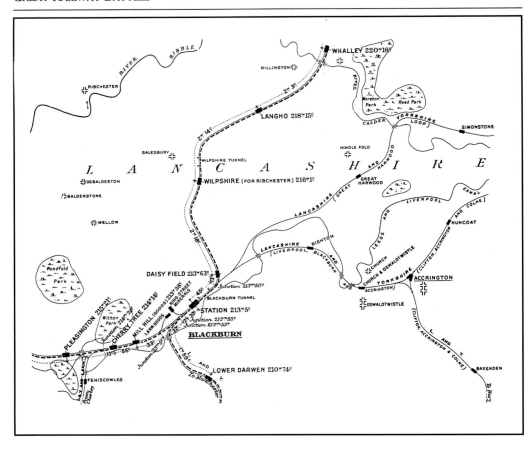

Railways serving Blackburn; the upper map is taken from the Midland Railway Distance Diagrams.

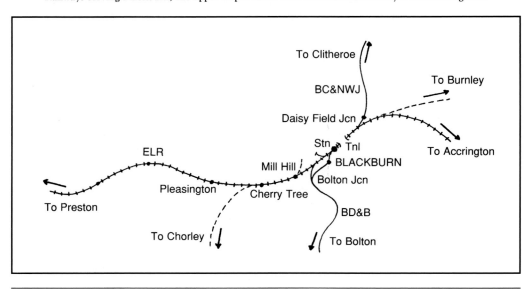

to lose out again in the near future, for work on the Blackburn's route north to Chatburn was nearing completion and, once it was ready, the Clitheroe traffic, which the ELR had been carrying by coach connections to and from the trains calling at Accrington, would also be lost to its rival.

Another blow fell early in 1850 when an agreement was announced between the Blackburn company and the Lancashire & Yorkshire Railway. The latter was to take over the working of the BBC&WY from 6 March and establish a management committee that would permit the smaller company to be operated as if it were an integral part of its larger neighbour. This meant, in effect, that once the line to Chatburn was completed the L&Y would be working traffic over the section of line through the ELR's station

and tunnel at Blackburn. L&Y trains would not only be providing a faster service from Manchester and threatening to go beyond Chatburn in the future, but also working through the ELR heartland at Blackburn itself; a recipe for trouble.

The situation on the ground at Blackburn at this time was that the Bolton line arrived from Darwen well to the west of the town, and ran parallel with the ELR line from Preston to a station in Great Bolton Street, where the Blackburn Railway had its headquarters and which later became the goods depot. The two routes made junction about 440 yards east of the present Bolton Junction, then continued through the ELR station and Blackburn Tunnel to Daisy Field Junction where the Clitheroe/Chatburn line departed for the Ribble valley.

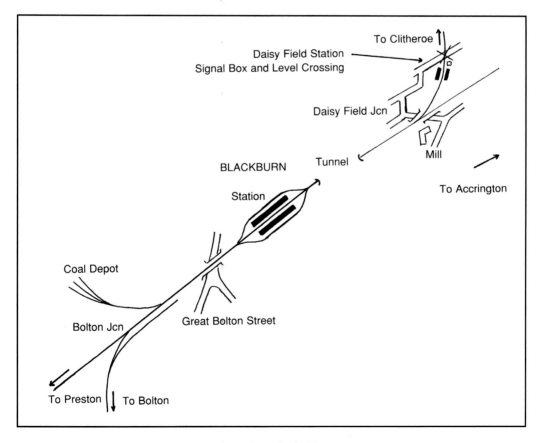

Railways through Blackburn.

As the works on the Chatburn line first surmounted a period of financial stringency, then neared completion, the rival railways began to think about the problems associated with the communal use of Blackburn station, and about the tolls to be raised for working over the ELR line between Bolton and Daisy Field junctions. On 12 February 1850 the BBC&WY suggested to the ELR that a committee should be formed to agree terms. The latter agreed, but neither party did anything further until the ELR was again approached on 29 March with a request for its terms. These were sent on 9 April, but shocked the Blackburn company with the suggestion that it should pay a toll equal to 6 miles when the actual distance involved was less than 1 mile. The toll payable to the ELR did, of course, need to compensate that company for its provision of signalling and station facilities as well as for the use of the track, but the level chosen was excessive and doubtless reflected the state of relations between the rival railways.

The Blackburn company took only three days to reject the ELR suggestion, but at that time made no counter-proposals. The ELR waited until 16 May, then served formal notice that it was referring the matter to arbitration. The arbitrators appointed by the Railway Commissioners first met on 9 June and immediately afterwards the East Lancashire's general manager, C. W. Eborall, met Terence Flanagan, now the BBC&WY manager and engineer. Eborall put forward the suggestion that the smaller company should pay the 6-mile toll then receive a refund if, when a decision was finally made, the award proved to be lower. It was later alleged that whereas the Blackburn company would have expected this to be upon completion of arbitration, the East Lancashire company meant at the end of any legal action it might see fit to take in pursuance of its point of view. This differing viewpoint also led to the ELR rejection of an offer by the BBC&WY directors to give their personal guarantee for any monies to which the ELR might ultimately be entitled, and to make a deposit to support this.

Blackburn Tunnel, seen from the east end of Blackburn station.

On 12 June the BBC&WY decided to test the position physically and turned out a light engine with the company's engineer on the footplate. The engine left Great Bolton Street station and moved through the junction towards the ELR station, but then found that the latter company had reacted more quickly than anticipated and had blocked the line between the end of the platform and the mouth of the tunnel with a light engine of its own. The ELR staff would not permit the intruder to proceed. With one of its trains bound for Accrington and Manchester waiting to depart, that company's officials put increasing pressure on the BBC&WY staff, who had little option but to give way and take their engine back the way it had come.

On the following day, the 13th, the Blackburn company's solicitors formally rejected the idea of paying the toll demanded on promise of a refund, and proceedings went ahead for the opening of the Chatburn line without any resolution of the vital issue in dispute between the ELR and BBC&WY concerns. General manager Eborall fixed up a meeting with Terence Flanagan for 21 June, but Mr Flanagan was tied up with the preparations for the formal opening of the Clitheroe line on the preceding day, Thursday 20 June, and in preparing for public running from Saturday, the 22nd of the month.

The ceremonial opening of the new railway went off well enough, with full ELR co-operation and no sign of the storm to come. There was a 15-coach train from Manchester, which arrived at the ELR station without hindrance at noon, then went forward to Clitheroe to load up its first official guests and return to Blackburn. It departed thence for Whalley at 2 pm, the privileged passengers there enjoying a 'splendid fete' which had been laid on to celebrate the event. The lucky guests had a tour of Whalley Abbey and the usual cold collation as a prelude to listening to the formal speeches and relaxing again with music and dancing before the final journey back to Blackburn.

The affairs of the Saturday were considerably less happy. The early train of empty stock from Blackburn to Clitheroe met with no hindrance, but there was trouble ahead

for its back working as the 8.20 am public service through to Manchester. As the *Blackburn Standard* reported, 'it was found that a complete blockade of the points had been effected at the junction with the East Lancashire Railway, near Turners Mill at Daisyfield, and that upwards of 200 navvies had been brought on the ground by the East Lancashire Company with several engines and a heavy train of stone wagons'. Here was a virtual repeat of the Clifton Junction incident with engines, a stone train and attendant navvies, but this time with the East Lancashire Railway as the aggressor.

Mind you, general manager Eborall put the facts differently in a subsequent defensive but reasoned letter to the newspaper. He wrote:

'On the morning of opening when the collector attended to receive the toll at the junction this was paid for the second train after some hesitation; when it had passed some observations were communicated to him which had been made on the previous night by parties connected with the Bolton company and some threats made that morning of a determination to pass over the railway by force without payment of the toll which, coupled with the threat of a solicitor's letter to stop our traffic, led to fear of violence. Only then, and when passengers were being dropped short of the junction, were workmen brought on site'.

The latter phrase is a reference to the fact that, after the early trains, subsequent BBC&WY services were stopped to pick up and discharge passengers where the line crossed Moss Street, just ahead of the Daisy Field Junction. They were then worked through Blackburn empty and ran round, by this expedient avoiding any liability for toll!

The confrontation at Daisy Field Junction appears to have continued throughout the Saturday with no trains getting through the blockade once it had been reinstated. At some stage there seems to have been an offer to pay the toll, and some time during the day the resident Blackburn magistrates, apprehensive for the peace of the district, signed a memorial and despatched it to the Railway Commissioners setting out the dangerous and unsatisfactory situation and requesting urgent action on the dispute. But even this measure of disapproval failed to bring a change in the ELR attitude, and the obstruction was maintained until late on the Saturday evening when the BBC&WY finally gave in and sent an undertaking, via Captain Laws of the L&Y, that it would pay the toll demanded. The three Sunday services were allowed to operate normally upon payment of the 6-mile toll, but in a formal communication between Captain Laws and the East Lancashire concern on the Monday, the former warned that 'a game had been commenced at which two companies might very well play'. This could have been little else but a reminder of the Clifton Junction affair and notice that it might well be repeated. However, for the time being the ELR had made its point, and the BBC&WY services were allowed to operate normally upon payment of the requisite toll.

Some idea of the bitter feeling between the parties is apparent in the letter which Terence Flanagan wrote to the local newspaper, to counter the one written by the ELR general manager. In a marvellous piece of rambling vituperation he maintained that he had 'waded through Mr Eborall's lucubrations from beginning to end' and went on:

'. . .and I have no hesitation, without entering more fully into particulars than I have done, in declaring that there is not one single statement contained in them which is not either garbled, distorted or positively incorrect; and he omits altogether any mention of the vexation and unprecedented proceedings on the part of the East Lancashire Company, which he well knows would be hopeless, with the greatest efforts of his pen, either to justify or palliate in the eyes of an impartial public.'

Terence Flanagan had been deeply involved in the building of the line from Preston to Blackburn, but any loyalty he may once have had to the ELR had now completely disappeared.

Another light on the feelings engendered by the rivalry between the two railways comes from the advertising of the new railway facility. In the same issue as the 'Railway Blockade' report, the *Blackburn Standard* carried an advertisement under the Lancashire & Yorkshire Railway imprint and the head-

The level crossing and signal box in Moss Street, Blackburn, with the platform of Daisy Field station just beyond.

ing 'Manchester, Blackburn, Darwen, Clitheroe and Whalley District', stating:

'The public is respectfully informed that the extension line to Clitheroe including Chatburn, Settle etc, the beautiful valley of the Ribble and the ancient ruins of the abbeys of Whalley and Sawley, together with the picturesque scenery of Whitewell, Stoneyhurst and neighbourhood is open for public traffic on Saturday June 22nd 1850. This is the only route by which passengers can book through, without change of carriage, to and from Clitheroe, Whalley, Chatburn etc via Bolton.'

The notice went on to detail the four through services daily between Manchester (Salford) and Chatburn plus one Blackburn-Chatburn service and the three trains each way on Sundays.

Throughout the rest of June and the whole of August the L&Y was forced to operate the BBC&WY line trains under the duress of paying the 6-mile toll for their journey through Blackburn. No doubt this left a bitter taste, but peace came at last on 16 September when the arbitrators finally made their decision. This awarded the ELR a 2-mile toll for the use of the running powers through the station, plus the right to charge at cost for the provision of points, signals and the staff to operate them. Despite the conflict that had taken place, talk of amalgamation had also been in the air, and the two rivals did, at least, go on to develop a working agreement that eased some of the tensions between them.

Curiously, the ultimate solution in this dispute was very similar to that in the Clifton Junction case, viz the joint acquisition by the ELR and L&Y of the line at the centre of the quarrel, but more muddy water had to flow under the bridge before this finally came about. The BBC&WY had retained its independent existence despite the L&Y working arrangement and, when relations between the ELR and L&Y concerns began to improve in 1854, the Blackburn company found itself under attack from them both!

The new allies started to divert Blackburn traffic via Preston or Accrington instead of Bolton, but after suffering this for a while, the Blackburn Railway made a splendid counter-attack on 28 August 1856 by promoting its own access to Manchester in the shape of a Bill for a new line via Whitefield. The L&Y successfully opposed this measure, but then found itself sued for loss of traffic by its former protégé, which showed every sign of presenting the offending measure again. In desperation the L&Y offered to buy the Blackburn company and, although the latter put up a tremendous fight, it was eventually forced into amalgamation with its two larger rivals, effective from 1 January 1858, confirmed by the L&Y Act of 12 July, and with the Bolton Road station at Blackburn being closed in favour of the ELR one. With the amalgamation of the ELR and L&Y following, the bitter enmity of Clifton Junction and Daisy Field Junction was at last over. The East Lancashire was to retain some identity as a separate division within the L&Y until 1913, when the system introduced central control at Manchester Victoria. The East Lancashire Division provided the L&Y with a general manager in 1864 and doubtless this did much to finalise the process of healing the wounds of the earlier years.

In recent years a curious reminder of the whole affair came with the 1987 restoration of a spasmodic passenger service to the Clitheroe line. Following this trains once again passed from the old BBC&WY line on to the ex-ELR line at Daisy Field Junction, approaching it via the level crossing in Moss Street, Blackburn, where passengers had been set down on the day of the 1850 dispute to make their own way into town and avoid the toll. On through Daisy Field station, which closed on 3 November 1958, the restored services cross the bridge over Fort Street and join the Accrington line under the shadow of Turners Mill before entering the tunnel and eventually emerging just before Blackburn station. Beyond the latter the route crosses over Great Bolton Street, where the BBC&WY had its own station, before the BR Bolton and Preston lines separate at Bolton Junction.

11
OUTBREAK OF WAR

The scheme for a railway between London and York provoked some of the bitterest opposition in early railway history, mainly from the established trunk line to the north, that of the London & Birmingham Railway and its LNWR successor. By its alliances with other major railways, notably the Midland, and its use of every conceivable tactic of obstruction, the LNWR sought tirelessly and without shame to limit the growth of the line it considered an upstart. As a result, the project that became the Great Northern Railway encountered a level of hostility without parallel in railway history. It became involved in a war that was to last for 13 years and produce the series of dirty and devious campaigns described in this and subsequent chapters.

The initial opposition of rival schemes, established carriers and intransigent landowners resulted in the London & York promoters being defeated in the 1845 session of Parliament and severely mauled in that of 1846. In the former the embryo Great Northern Railway lost its Wakefield and Sheffield branches during the Commons readings, these being postponed for future consideration on the grounds that rival plans needed to be taken into account. Things did go better for the main scheme in 1846, but the Act finally passed on 26 June cut out most of the remaining branches when it approved plans for the main line to York and the loop line through Lincoln. A small compensation was the authorisation of the Boston-Grimsby line of the East Lincolnshire

> **Protagonists:**
> Great Northern Railway with Euston Square Confederacy members, and Manchester, Sheffield & Lincolnshire Railway
>
> **Location:**
> Methley Junction, Retford and Grimsby stations
>
> **Date:**
> 1849-1851

Railway, which was to be leased to the Great Northern.

Also significant in the 1846 session was the approval of the Manchester & Leeds Railway's scheme for a line from a junction with the GN at Askern to one with the Midland Railway at Methley, and of the Sheffield & Lincolnshire Extension Railway's (MS&LR from 1846) plans for a connection from the Sheffield & Lincolnshire Junction (MS&L) Retford-Gainsborough line to the GN's Lincoln-Gainsborough line at Sykes Junction, Saxilby.

The Great Northern response to the loss of its branches was to endeavour to establish alliances that would produce the same result. One such alliance was with the Manchester & Leeds, firstly to secure running powers over that company's newly authorised line from Askern to Methley, and secondly for inclusion, with the M&L and the Leeds &

Thirsk and Leeds & Dewsbury companies, in a scheme for a central station at Leeds. The 1847 Parliamentary session rejected GN extensions from the L&Y line to Leeds and Wakefield, primarily owing to technical errors in their submission, but did approve the Leeds station plan, a schedule to the Act confirming the GN's running powers to Methley. The GNR was now significantly closer to reaching Leeds, an objective important for its traffic potential and also, one suspects, because it was the chairman's home town!

Another development in 1847, the year in which the M&L became part of the Lancashire & Yorkshire Railway, was a Great Northern agreement with the Midland Railway under which the latter gave the former running powers on from Methley to Leeds. Signed by George Hudson on 16 October, this agreement was more to exercise some control over the GN trains than to facilitate their incursion into the Hudson empire. Compared with the alternative of a re-submission of the GN scheme for independent access to Leeds, it did at least provide the MR with some revenue from tolls as well as giving that company the whip hand in operational matters.

By virtue of its lease of the East Lincolnshire Railway the Great Northern was able to earn its first revenue from 1 March 1848 with services from Louth to New Holland. Trains ran over the ELR line from Louth as far as Grimsby, then continued to New Holland, and a connection with the Hull steamers, under an agreement to use the MS&L onward section as part of a shared service. By 30 June just over £2,500 had been earned, but this was small beer compared with the £2.5 million already spent on construction work.

A nasty blow fell in March when Parliament postponed the Deviation Bill for routing the GN 'loop line' to Doncaster via Rossington instead of Bawtry. This loop line, from Peterborough via Boston and Lincoln, had been started before the main line because it was easiest and could earn money quickly, but the deviation at the Doncaster end was an important improvement on the

original line of route and its temporary rejection a serious hindrance. The solution proved to lie in an extension of the alliance with the MS&L, that company being persuaded to bring forward the building of its link from Clarborough (east of Retford) to Saxilby, a proposal that had originally been planned to give the MS&L a route into Lincoln in return for GN running powers to Sheffield. With the GN hurriedly letting a contract for Peto & Betts to build the Retford-Doncaster section, this piece of co-operation would now fit in well with the GN's plans and allow completion of a through route from Peterborough to Doncaster, albeit via Boston, Lincoln and Retford.

Other developments in 1848 included the ELR opening from Firsby to Louth on 3 September, with completion through to Boston on 1 October. Sixteen days later the 58 miles from Peterborough to Lincoln via Boston was opened and Lincoln passengers were able to cut an hour off the journey to London by travelling on the newly opened line, using a short stretch of the MR to reach the Eastern Counties line at Peterborough, then continuing over that company's system to Shoreditch, London. The Great Northern was now becoming the real threat that its opponents had feared. And that threat gained even more substance when Hudson agreed to its use of a Knottingley to Burton Salmon connection to reach the York & North Midland, and thus save the cost of separate access to York.

Beyond Doncaster the L&Y had been able to work over the Askern Junction-Doncaster section to bring racegoers to the September 1848 meetings, and the GNR was looking forward to a large share of this race traffic revenue in 1849. The Lincoln-Gainsborough section had opened on 9 April and this was followed on 4 September by the Doncaster-Retford portion, which, added to the MS&L's Clarborough-Sykes Junction branch, meant that services from Peterborough and Leeds could be introduced. The Midland was duly advised of the intention to operate such services from 4 September, but declined to agree unless the GN formally abandoned its hopes for inde-

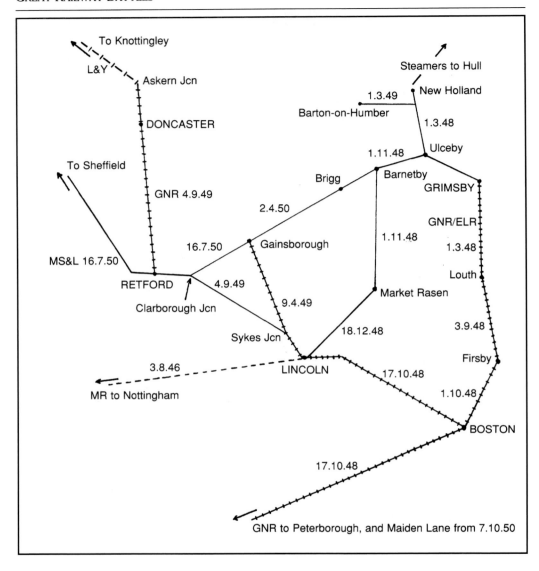

To Knottingley

L&Y

Askern Jcn

DONCASTER

To Sheffield

GNR 4.9.49

MS&L 16.7.50

16.7.50

RETFORD

Clarborough Jcn

4.9.49

3.8.46

MR to Nottingham

Sykes Jcn

9.4.49

LINCOLN

Gainsborough

2.4.50

Brigg

18.12.48

17.10.48

17.10.48

Steamers to Hull

New Holland

1.3.49

Barton-on-Humber

1.3.48

Ulceby

1.11.48

Barnetby

GRIMSBY

GNR/ELR

1.11.48

1.3.48

Market Rasen

Louth

3.9.48

Firsby

1.10.48

BOSTON

GNR to Peterborough, and Maiden Lane from 7.10.50

Great Northern and MS&L lines in and around Lincolnshire, with opening dates.

pendent access to Leeds. Unless this was conceded the MR threatened to stop all GN trains at Methley and demand the maximum toll for every passenger on board! The covert opposition of the past was now coming out into the open.

The Great Northern, determined not to be intimidated, went on planning for the new Leeds service and for the Doncaster race specials that would bring in much-needed income. As the South Yorkshire Railway's line from Swinton was also open and the Midland able to exercise running powers over it, that company, too, expected much of the racing business.

In its issue of Friday 7 September 1849 the *Doncaster Chronicle & Farmers Journal* reported that 'the preparations which annually precede the Doncaster Races are now drawing to a close. The inns, betting-rooms, and private

New Holland station in GCR days. *Lens of Sutton*

houses, are for the most part ready to receive their respective visitors. . .'

The newspaper's 'Local Intelligence' also revealed that the Midland Railway's threats had not been idle ones, announcing:

'Atrocious Conduct in a
Railway Company

It is incredible to what lengths the blind passions of great public companies will lead them. The public narrowly escaped a frightful catastrophe on Tuesday, in the opening of the Great Northern line, when the trains were about to run from Doncaster to Leeds. The Superintendent at Doncaster, having heard it whispered that something was going on at the junction of the Doncaster line with the Midland Railway at Methley, sent over a special engine before the trains and found the servants of the Midland Company had removed the points at the junction, so that had the train proceeded thither it would inevitably run off the road. This, we understand, was done without any notice, in consequence of some dispute between the two companies, for which the Midland Company

would have made the lives of her Majesty's subjects pay. Such an outrage must surely meet with due punishment.'

Both the Great Northern and the Lancashire & Yorkshire protested vehemently at this arbitrary action, but it was to be 1 October before the matter was fully resolved and the Great Northern trains could finally abandon their roundabout alternative via Wakefield and run through to Leeds via Methley junction without hindrance. To achieve this end the agreement of 16 October 1847 had to be produced and legal action threatened, but, ironically, the strength of the former was somewhat undermined by the fact that Hudson had already resigned in disgrace from the Midland on 17 April.

Although the Leeds access problem had been settled for the time being and the Great Northern had, in 1849, earned its first real profit of just over £10,000, other problems were now looming. This time the attack was to come from its MS&L partner, which had been described in an 1849 directors' report as labouring 'under the combined evils of defective traffic, insufficient capital, injured credit and a disunited proprietary'. The meagre

93

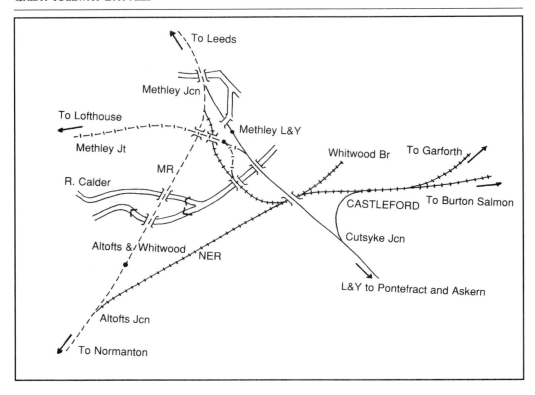

Lines and junctions at Methley.

The Midland-pattern signal box at Methley Junction in 1993.

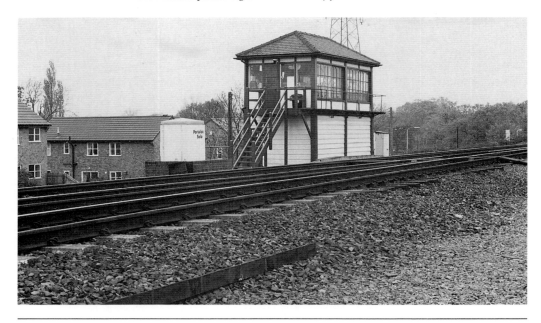

half-year profit of £22,576 had all gone to pay off creditors, and with no dividend to offer, the company was in dire straits.

Up to this time the GN/MS&L co-operation on the ground had worked well enough, although subject to the raw operational problems that bedeviled all the early companies. A picture of such railway activity at Retford is painted, again by the *Doncaster Chronicle*, in an article that first describes a sad accident in which a guard was run over by a train from Manchester at 10 o'clock, and then continues:

'Within two hours after this had occurred, another accident happened which might have been attended with the most fatal consequences. A train had arrived from Gainsbro', and was upon its regular line, when the special train from London to Doncaster (for the races) arrived. Both had here to take in water. Unfortunately, a porter of the name of Barker interfered, and turned one of the points, whereby the Doncaster engine and train came into contact with the Sheffield train, and the consequence was that the engine and two carriages were thrown completely off the rails. Fortunately the engine driver of the London train saw the danger, and with the greatest alacrity and presence of mind, shut off the steam, and reversed the engine, otherwise the whole train would have gone slap through the other. The passengers appeared much frightened, but none of them were injured. After some delay the engine was got on to the rails again, and proceeded on its course to Doncaster.'

The importation of James Allport from the York, Newcastle & Berwick Railway to tackle the MS&L's wider difficulties coincided with a decision of the Euston group of railways to court the cross-country company in order to weaken the threat posed by the Great Northern activity, especially in relation to access over the MS&L to Manchester. As its general manager designate, Allport represented the MS&L inter-

ests at a meeting attended by LNW, Midland and L&Y representatives on 5 December 1849. In place of its long-standing tactic of diverting traffic away from the MS&L, the Euston group was now offering to route goods and passengers via the ailing system and to recognise that it should have a monopoly of all the business flowing to and from Hull. All the MS&L had to do in return was to withdraw its goodwill from the Great Northern and afford it no more assistance than it was obliged to.

The temptation was too much for the near-bankrupt provincial undertaking and, after two further meetings to hammer out the details, its directors met on 16 January 1850 and endorsed an alliance that placed it squarely in the Euston group and repudiated its former relationship with the GNR. Specifically, the MS&L had to agree to limit the Great Northern's facilities for the Hull traffic passing via New Holland, and to divert all the traffic it could from the GNR to the Midland route via Lincoln. The Euston group's fears for its Manchester business were covered by a requirement that the MS&L was to make no arrangements with the GN for such traffic. A further clause specifically provided that should the Great Northern avail itself of its Parliamentary powers to work over the MS&L line to Sheffield, that company was to charge maximum rates and give 'no accommodation or facilities which they were not bound to afford under existing Acts of Parliament'.

The MS&L defection, timed with a cynical eye on the progress of the GN link from Peterborough to London, was to unleash a period of total attrition between the Great Northern Railway and its neighbours. The Midland and L&Y companies refused to exchange traffic at Leeds and Wakefield, and the MS&L followed suit at Grimsby and Retford. The GN retaliated by hindering the latter's traffic access to Lincoln rather than see everything diverted to the Midland's route from there. Further away, the Eastern Counties Railway was even persuaded to delay building the onward link from Shepreth to Cambridge and to route its Peterborough exchanges via the Midland's

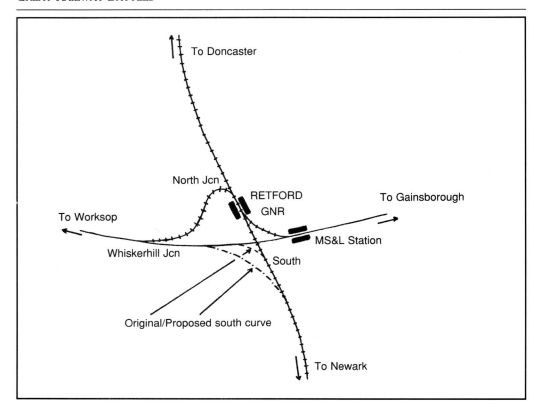

To Doncaster

North Jcn

RETFORD
GNR

To Gainsborough

To Worksop

MS&L Station

Whiskerhill Jcn

South

Original/Proposed south curve

To Newark

Left Stations and junctions at Retford.

Below left Typical Great Northern buildings survive at Retford up side, although over-large for present-day requirements.

Above right Instead of crossing the main line on the level, as it did in Great Northern days, the ex-MS&L/GC line to Sheffield now passes beneath it.

Right Retford North Junction today: Civil Engineer's machine DR 73435 moves forward from the down side depot.

Syston line. The only bright spot for the Great Northern was that the York & North Midland Railway kept faith with its agreement for access to York via the Knottingley-Burton Salmon link.

On behalf of the MS&L Allport seemed to feel obliged to implement his commitment to his Euston partners to the full. At Retford GN services could still work forward to Doncaster via the connecting spur between the two routes, but prohibitive tolls were imposed on access to Sheffield. The co-operation that had previously existed was suddenly withdrawn, and GN trains could no longer take water at the MS&L station before passing over the curve to their own. New facilities had to be improvised in a hurry.

Grimsby became the centre of further acrimony, especially after the failure of a 5-year

peace deal offered by Lord Yarborough, the MS&L chairman, in May 1850. The 1848 agreement for through working to New Holland and the Hull steamers steadily crumbled, until first GN locomotives were excluded from the MS&L section, then all passengers from the East Lincolnshire line were compelled to change trains. On at least one occasion the MS&L staff placed obstructions on the track to enforce their sanctions. At the height of the dispute Hull steamers were allowed to leave New Holland before the GN passengers had reached there, forcing the luckless travellers to spend the night in their trains or in the station waiting room.

In a celebrated court case arising out of the dispute between the MS&L and GN railways, a Mr Hamlin, who had missed appointments in Hull as a result of the railway

Grimsby station was the frontier between the GNR and MS&L systems. It is seen here in 1993, still with its overall roof, viewed from the west, MS&L, end.

At the other end of the station is Garden Street signal box and barrier crossing, with the old East Lincs Junction beyond.

antics, sued the Great Northern for failing to convey him to his destination in a reasonable time. He did get compensation for his overnight stay in Grimsby, but the judge ruled that Hamlin's proper course when he found the New Holland train gone would have been to have hired a cab to chase after it!

With the opening of its line to London on 7 June 1850 the Great Northern had become a major contender for the trunk route business, despite all the petty restrictions imposed by its adversaries. With them it was looking forward to a boost in revenue from the opening of the Great Exhibition on 1 May 1851, the railway intention being to offer cheap fares for travel to this incredible event from the beginning of July. To avoid a fares free-for-all the GN put forward proposals for the pooling of receipts on competitive traffic flows south of York in the February, but the rival companies could not agree and asked Mr Gladstone to arbitrate. Pending his decision they patched up a temporary arrangement that quickly broke down and led to a period of fantastic bargains and indescribable travel scenes before Gladstone's decisions in August restored some sanity to the matter. His ruling vindicated the GN position with an award of 63 per cent of the traffic arising at six important towns.

The autumn of 1851 also saw the revival of the former West Riding Union scheme in the shape of a Leeds, Bradford & Halifax Junction Railway Bill, involving a link from Leeds to Bowling and supported by the GN to develop its penetration westwards. This was too much for Captain Laws of the L&Y, formerly a good friend of the Great Northern and with a seat on its board. Laws gave up the latter and his company gave formal notice that the right to run to Methley and Wakefield would be withdrawn unless the GN agreed to pay the full Parliamentary toll.

Around this time the MS&L advised the Great Northern that it was to withdraw the Grimsby-New Holland facilities altogether.

The combination of the Gladstone awards and successful Great Northern suits in Chancery against the L&Y and MS&L restrictions brought a measure of peace to this first phase of the combat between the new trunk route and its neighbours. But the whole issue was to crop up again when the Six Towns fares agreement expired at the end of five years and, meantime, further trouble had broken out in East Anglia and was brewing in Nottingham.

The scenes of this front-line obstruction in 1850-51 are much more peaceful today. At Methley the L&Y section on from Castleford to the junction has gone, although its course is marked by the bridge over the Aire & Calder Navigation and by the station house at Methley L&Y. Trains from Castleford to Leeds follow the old NER route and join the freight-only ex-Midland line from Altofts Junction at Methley Junction, where the surviving signal box is reached by a lane from the A639 road.

Retford has changed dramatically. The former MS&L line, which for many years crossed the GN main line on the level, now burrows beneath it, and a new low-level station is reached by walking the length of the ECML up main platform. The route of the spur up towards the main line is barely discernible, while the south spur has gone altogether. The two routes are still connected by a single line round from Retford North Junction to meet the rising Sheffield line as it regains its level after the underpass. Grimsby, on the other hand, has changed much less than the other locations, but while one can still travel on to New Holland the days of the paddle-steamer ferries across to Hull Corporation Pier are now just a memory.

12
REVOLT AT NEWMARKET

Not all the railway battles involved physical confrontation. Some contained the same elements of force and bullying but within the commercial conventions of the day. The cunning and hostility displayed in such cases was often just as intense as in those involving face-to-face aggression, but the period over which it applied was usually significantly longer and some regard, at least, was paid to appearances.

A classic case of respectable, on-going aggression was that which brought about the swallowing up of the Newmarket Railway by its larger Eastern Counties Railway neighbour. To some extent, also, the Newmarket was a victim of its own ambitions, but the case revealed a fascinating mix of the hopes, ploys, successes and failures that abounded in the conflicts of the early railway years.

The period involved was a turbulent one in which the Eastern Counties company, although early on the East Anglian railway scene, still had to face the fact that many other railways were being promoted and all wanted either extensive, quick and profitable growth or a good take-over offer. The conflict inherent in this situation was heightened by the 1845 election to the chair of the Eastern Counties board of George Hudson, then being called the 'Railway King' for his empire-building proclivity. Under Hudson's influence the ECR, despite a precarious financial position, saw itself not only as dominating East Anglia but also providing a successful challenge to the infant London & York scheme, later the Great Northern

Protagonists:
Eastern Counties Railway and
Newmarket Railway

Location:
Newmarket-Cambridge area

Date:
1849-1851

Railway. At a meeting on 30 October 1845, just 17 days after accepting the ECR chair, Hudson was proposing an extension north through Lincoln and Doncaster, which, together with the link to Peterborough, would bring the company rich traffic dividends.

The Eastern Counties Railway had already taken a lease of the pioneer Northern & Eastern railway project, and on 29 July 1845 it extended the N&E line from Bishops Stortford, north via Cambridge and Ely, then east to Brandon. There a junction was made with the Norfolk Railway's line, and following the completion of Trowse swing-bridge at Norwich on 15 December 1845, trains could operate right through from Shoreditch to Yarmouth. The 146-mile journey took just over 6 hours, but, while tapping some important traffic centres and taking the ECR nearer to a link with the rest of Hudson's empire, it was overly circuitous for the Norfolk business.

The ECR's other, and original, main line

had reached Colchester on 29 March 1843, but had then run out of funds, the mantle of taking the route forward being donned by the Eastern Union Railway, which eventually reached Bury St Edmunds in 1846 and Norwich in 1849. The scene facing Hudson was thus one of a newly completed main line already under challenge for the Norwich business, while in the Kings Lynn area the Lynn & Ely, Lynn & Dereham and Ely & Huntingdon companies were on the point of amalgamating as the East Anglian Railway and represented another threat to the ECR's plans for domination. The battle that resulted from the emergence of the EAR group and its alliance with the Great Northern Railway is described in the next chapter.

Although a year of achievement, 1845 brought another possible rival to trouble the Eastern Counties' fragile lead in the railway stakes. This took the form of the Newmarket & Chesterford Railway, which issued its prospectus for a 16³/₄-mile main line from Newmarket to Great Chesterford and an 8¹/₂-mile branch from Six Mile Bottom to Cambridge. The cost of construction was expected to be £350,000, which was to be funded by the issue of £25 shares; Robert Stephenson and John Braithwaite were the engineers, and the scheme had the advantage of support from the Jockey Club. Some idea of the aspirations behind the new railway can be obtained from the expression of that support, viz:

'The Jockey Club felt that a railway to Newmarket would not only be a great convenience to parties anxious to participate in the truly British sport of racing but would enable Members of Parliament to superintend a race and run back to London in time for the same night's debate.'

By October 1845 an abridged Newmarket & Chesterford prospectus was able to state that the number of shares applied for was 'so numerous that applications cannot be attended to, except from parties locally interested'. Letters of allotment were issued on 1 November.

On 16 July 1846 the Newmarket & Chesterford Railway Act received the Royal Assent, with £350,000 authorised capital and borrowing powers of £116,666 13s 4d. With the support of the Jockey Club, and with Lord George Manners, son of the fifth Duke of Rutland, as chairman of its Committee of Management, the new railway scheme had not been troubled by opposition and had spent only £2,000 in obtaining its legislation. With a contract for construction let to a Mr Jackson, the first sod was cut at Dullingham on 30 September by the 10-year-old Master Jeaffreson, accompanied by Lord George and the usual festivities.

The new railway had not only wasted no time in starting the construction process, but had also followed its successful approach to Parliament with an immediate proposal to the Norfolk Railway that it should take the N&C on lease at a rental of 6 per cent on the authorised capital. This was a remarkably rapid attempt to get rich quick, the N&C management already seeing their railway as part of a shorter route to Norfolk and placing a high value on that attribute. But the move was too early and the Norfolk Railway, valuing the reality of its existing link with the ECR at Brandon and only anxious to enhance its potential take-over value in the eyes of that company, came to a second meeting and said that it could not proceed without the ECR's approval.

Some talks had already been held with the Eastern Counties itself in view of the junction to be made with the latter's main line at Great Chesterford, and the N&C chairman now reported that the larger company was prepared to lease the Newmarket undertaking for 999 years at a rental of 5 per cent on the £350,000 capital, plus a share in the profits after they had risen above the £17,500 rental figure. However, a shattering blow fell on the aspiring N&C just 48 hours before a meeting on 11 November 1846, called to ratify the ECR agreement, when that company too pulled back from the brink, maintaining that the N&C had misinterpreted the terms of the proposed agreement.

No one seemed to want to provide the N&C with a comfortable and guaranteed liv-

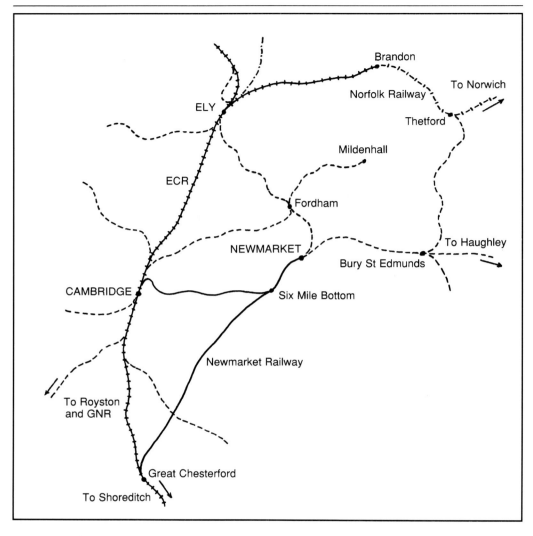

The Newmarket Railway (formerly Newmarket & Chesterford) and surrounding lines.

ing. Obeying the maxim about attack being the best form of defence, the Newmarket company therefore retaliated to these rejections by placing orders for £88,000 worth of engines, carriages and trucks so that it could run its railway without reliance on either the Norfolk or Eastern Counties concerns. Boldly it approached Parliament for an extension to Bury with a branch to Ely, and for a line from Newmarket to Thetford, also securing permission to simplify its name to just Newmarket Railway. By 10 August 1847 the

directors had agreed on yet another new line, this time to meet the Royston & Hitchin concern, which the Great Northern had agreed to lease on completion. In the wider sphere the Eastern Union had by now reached Bury St Edmunds and the East Anglian had reached Ely. The railway activities around Cambridge were becoming volatile and interesting, especially in view of this new possibility of a connection with the GN network.

On 3 January 1848 the Newmarket

Railway opened its line between Newmarket and Great Chesterford for goods traffic, using its own locomotives and a small initial supply of trucks. By the following month a meeting was reporting that although the Eastern Counties Goliath was unwilling to reach any accommodation with the Newmarket David, extension to Thetford was again under consideration, and provisional agreement had been reached with the Norfolk Railway to work the whole route from Thetford through to Great Chesterford and to route its London business, worth some £40,000 a year, that way. This must have caused great anxiety in the Eastern Counties camp raising, as it did, the real prospect of a new route to Norwich significantly shorter than the existing one via Cambridge. The development rapidly produced a counter-offer from the ECR, which was considered at a Newmarket Railway meeting on 27 March and agreed.

Temporarily, at least, relationships

Two views looking north from Great Chesterford towards the site of the N&C junction, with trees and bushes marking the course of the long-abandoned Newmarket route, which veered away right before the overbridge.

between the Newmarket and Eastern Counties concerns were now amicable enough for the introduction of passenger services from Newmarket to Great Chesterford and on to Shoreditch from 4 April 1848. Shortly afterwards the ECR removed the threat of a rival short-cut route to Norwich via Newmarket and Thetford by agreeing to take the Norfolk Railway on lease from 8 May. There was still another threat to face, however, for the Great Northern's creature, the Royston & Hitchin, now put forward a Bill for extension to Cambridge; and it would not have been difficult for the Newmarket concern to arrange a connection there.

Negotiations between the ECR and Newmarket companies continued during the summer of 1848, although these were not the only matters demanding the latter's attention. On 12 May, for example, the 3.30 pm mixed train from Newmarket was involved in a nasty incident. On arriving at Dullingham the brake-van was detached to allow some trucks to be picked up from the goods siding. The shunting process meant leaving coaches on the main line while the train engine went for the loaded wagons, but, as the former were not properly braked, they promptly ran back down the line towards Newmarket. There they smashed into the buffer stops of the ornate terminus with a crash that injured 44 people and produced a massive pile of wreckage.

The first financial results were now available to the Newmarket directors and showed that during the three months to 30 June 1848 earnings had totalled £3,085 7s 7d against expenses of £2,059 5s 7d. Since this represented a return of only 1 per cent on the capital outlay a committee of enquiry was appointed to examine the company's affairs. Its report proved critical, especially over the priority given to building the main line instead of concentrating on the local traffic that would have accrued from a link to Cambridge. Any lingering doubts about handing over the undertaking to the Eastern Counties were now set aside, and a lease was agreed with that company, operative from 3 October 1848 and based on a rental of 3 per cent for two years and an extra half per cent thereafter. The deal, although more modest

Railway Station, Newmarket.

A later Great Eastern Railway view of Newmarket station; only the GER could have assembled this rake of mixed stock! *Lens of Sutton*

than the heady ambitions of earlier talks, was still a good one. The ECR agreed to provide funds to liquidate the Newmarket liabilities and to complete the Cambridge branch, thus avoiding the need for the smaller company to make the final £5 call on its shares.

Both the East Anglian and the Newmarket Railway had opposed the Bill for the ECR's take-over of the Norfolk Railway, but Parliament had agreed to a lease, although approval for amalgamation was withheld. Now the Newmarket had fallen into the hands of the domineering ECR and the East Anglian was experiencing such increasing financial problems that it looked likely to follow suit. Not that the Newmarket was long to enjoy its new patronage, for 1849 was soon threatening to be a worse year than 1848.

The new year had hardly started when the Eastern Counties' own affairs were thrown into turmoil. George Hudson fell from grace and the Bill to legitimise the lease of the Newmarket Railway was rejected, partly because of the latter's capital shortcomings. In a rash of anti-Hudson hysteria the ECR company appointed its own committee of investigation, which reported, amongst other things, against the ECR lease of the Newmarket concern, and this was promptly repudiated. In a panic the Newmarket directors reopened discussions with the Norfolk Railway with proposals for the setting up of a joint working party and plans to route all Norfolk traffic via Thetford and Newmarket. But nothing had yet been done about building the connecting line between those two points and, with the Norfolk becoming increasingly dependent on the ECR, these moves, even if they were ever likely to come to anything, offered no prospect of solution to the short-term problems.

The Newmarket Railway was now in real trouble. Its former partner continued to work the line, but was charging the earth for the inferior level of service for which it was already notorious. In addition to an annual (mis)management charge of £600, the ECR was demanding 1s 5d per mile for the provision of locomotives against a level elsewhere of around half that figure. Worse, after originally rejecting the Newmarket engines and

rolling-stock, the ECR had finally agreed to take over these items at £20,480 down plus £29,520 to follow, making a total of £50,000 against the original cost of £88,000. So the smaller concern had thus lost £38,000 in the value of its assets as well as the means to operate its own services!

For the last period of 1848 the profit derived from the ECR's working of the main line amounted to only £704, and the larger company even hung on to that, maintaining that it might be required to settle claims between them! Revenue for the three months ended 30 June 1849 was £3,441, but the payment to the ECR for working the line was £3,668, adding a further loss for the Newmarket proprietors to worry about. At this time the smaller railway was still having to meet bond interest and to pay for the permanent way and stations out of its capital budget.

On 22 March 1849 the Newmarket directors set up another committee of investigation to look into its deteriorating affairs. Appointed to lead it was bankruptcy commissioner Cecil Fane, a former director who had resigned in disgust over the company's management. His report, made on 14 May, was highly critical and majored on the folly of completing the prestigious main line when that to Cambridge would have offered so much more in the way of traffic. It was proposed that the Cambridge line should be started forthwith, at an anticipated cost of £20,000 plus £15,000 for land, and the company should be worked by a new managing director under the supervision of five other directors.

With Jackson, the contractor, pressing to be paid and the debenture-holders adding their weight to the argument, the Newmarket Railway was in real trouble. In desperation the company even considered offering the working to Jackson, as its only remaining assets consisted of the undertaking itself and £2 left on the share calls. A final appeal was also made to the Eastern Counties, but to no avail, and the bitter decision had to be taken to suspend all services between Newmarket and Great Chesterford after 30 June 1850.

In these exceedingly gloomy circumstances and against all the odds a revival of the fighting spirit seemed to emerge. It all started at a meeting on 27 July 1850 when the directors defended their running of the company, but were roundly condemned by Fane and his group for neglecting the Cambridge line and for bungling the take-over negotiations. Amid popular acclaim Fane was elected to the chair and G. W. Brown, the company's secretary, was appointed as its manager. Between them these two were to work wonders during the months ahead, by

● persuading Jackson to knock £26,000 off his bill and to complete the Cambridge branch at a cost of not more than £9,000 - by the expedient of lifting one of the tracks from the main line;

● persuading the debenture-holders to reduce their interest, and telling defaulting shareholders that they must pay up or forfeit their shares;

● getting the Chancery suits settled by selling off unwanted land;

● getting the still unpaid rolling-stock builders to reduce their accounts; and

● completing negotiations with the ECR which would permit the use of the latter's Cambridge station.

All these efforts, coupled with a fresh Newmarket board and a new attitude towards the ECR, enabled the Newmarket Railway to borrow enough stock from the latter to reopen its route on 9 September 1850.

While all this drama was being enacted east of Cambridge, there were other developments to the west. The Royston & Hitchin was leased to the Great Northern from 1 August 1850 and opened on 21 October. By 1851 a Bill for separate access to Cambridge was before Parliament, and the reality of the Great Northern threat was soon to be underlined with the extension of the R&H line to Shepreth on 1 August 1851. By providing a daily service of five omnibuses from the latter point the GN then made its first inroads into the Cambridge traffic. The Bill for separate access to Cambridge and a connection to the Newmarket Railway was defeated, but at least prompted the ECR to complete the Shelford-Shepreth section and later to take the R&H on lease.

Not unmindful of the GN advance, the representatives of the Eastern Counties and Newmarket companies buried their differences in an agreement reached on 28 May 1851. In addition to allowing the Newmarket access to its Cambridge station, the ECR effectively reverted to a 3 per cent lease by undertaking to make good any revenue shortfall on this level up to an amount of £5,000 a year. After failing its inspection on 29 September owing to problems with the curve at Cambridge, the new Newmarket line obtained approval on 7 October, was opened the following day and began to carry public services from the 9th.

The new agreement was embodied in an Act of 1852 that authorised the ECR to purchase £25 Newmarket shares, written down to £15, using $3\frac{1}{2}$ per cent debentures payable three years hence. The ECR took over a Newmarket bond debt, which had reached the borrowing powers limit, and by 30 June 1854 had paid off £210,000 worth of debentures in cash. Including stamp duty, its small rival cost the ECR £326,923. Life now became a bit easier for the Newmarket proprietors and by February 1852 they had even been able to declare the company's first dividend, albeit a mere 1s 6d on each £25 share. Under ECR patronage work was started on the extension to Bury, and this was eventually opened on 1 April 1854, worked by the ECR for a rental of 5 per cent on the extra £145,000 of capital. The casualty in this contest was the original main line between Great Chesterford and Six Mile Bottom, closed the day the Cambridge branch started work. One track remained open, ostensibly for goods traffic, but there is no record of its use, and in 1858 Parliament sanctioned complete closure. There were later to be memorials urging the Great Eastern to reopen the neglected line, but nothing happened and the route gradually sank into oblivion.

A curve in the Cambridge line west of Six Mile Bottom is now the only mark of the divergence of the former N&C main line south towards Great Chesterford.

From today's electric trains heading north out of Great Chesterford station travellers can spot a line of trees burrowing into the embankment of the M11-A11 road link. This was once the site of the N&C junction, the old line itself heading off north-east through Bourn Bridge and Balsham Road stations on a course now paralleled by the A11, itself much modified over the years. At the other end of the abandoned section the original line met the Cambridge branch, without physical junction, just east of the road linking the A11 and Great Wilbraham village, the actual junction being located at Six Mile Bottom station. Today the remains of the slowly disappearing trackbed still bear their mute witness to the mistaken idea that the racing business would bring greater prosperity than local traffic to and from Cambridge. Standing on the remains of the abandoned line one might still, with a little imagination, visualise the early service of four trains each way hauled by Gilkes, Wilson & Co tender locomotives. These carried the names *Beeswing, Van Tromp, Queen of Trumps, Flying Dutchman, Eleanor* and *Alice Hawthorn*. The connection? They were all racehorses, of course!

13
THE EAST ANGLIAN AFFAIR

As the 19th century neared its halfway point the Great Northern Railway was well on the way to achieving its hard-fought ambitions. Its first revenue had been entered in the accounts for 1848, in the following year work began on the missing section of the main line between Peterborough and Retford, and in 1850 itself northbound trains would start running to and from a temporary London terminus at Maiden Lane. With the farsightedness that had characterised the undertaking since its inception, this period was also one of looking for branches and feeder lines that would bring business to the great trunk route nearing completion. But this policy had, as we have seen, already brought out the resentment of the company's neighbours to the north and west.

To the east the Eastern Counties Railway was emerging as the dominant force in East Anglia, but it was a patchwork affair and still had a number of rivals. George Hudson had become the company's chairman in 1845, bringing with him ambitions to link the ECR with the rest of his growing empire and a deep suspicion of his embryo Great Northern neighbour. The tensions between these two groups were later to come to a head at Wisbech, in the heart of the Fens.

Wisbech is an important Fenland market town standing on the River Nene, 11 miles from its entry to the Wash west of Kings Lynn. A medieval port, it achieved some early notoriety when King John lost a royal fortune nearby in 1216, but the draining of the Fenland marshes brought more worthy claims

> **Protagonists:**
> Eastern Counties Railway versus Great Northern and East Anglian railways
>
> **Location:**
> Wisbech, near the former Wisbech East station
>
> **Date:**
> 10 July 1851 to 1 January 1852

to notice as the agricultural exploitation of the rich soil led to a period of rapid commercial growth from about 1700 onwards. The merchants of the town built themselves some fine Georgian houses and took a sharp interest in anything that would supply the needs of the surrounding land or move its growing output to the tables of English homes. With the port handling over 150,000 tons of traffic each year and the area needing supplies of coal and bursting with marketable produce, Wisbech was early to excite the interest of railway promoters. Local lines were planned by the Wisbech, St Ives & Cambridge Junction Railway and by the Lynn & Ely Railway, the latter intending to reach the town by a branch from Watlington Road (later Magdalen Road). The WS&C, a satellite of the Hudson-dominated Eastern Counties Railway, opened its short, straight line from March on 3 May 1847, terminating at a station near the Nene at South Brink, Wisbech.

The year 1847 also saw the formation of the East Anglian Railway, an amalgam of the Lynn & Ely, Lynn & Dereham and Ely & Huntingdon concerns. The group had its origins in a meeting of Lynn townsfolk in 1844 under the chairmanship of Sir William Folkes, with its first enterprise, the Lynn & Ely, receiving its Act of Parliament on 30 June 1845. In addition to its 25-mile main line and a 1¼-mile Lynn Harbour branch, the company's 9½-mile branch from Watlington to Wisbech was originally intended to continue to March and Spalding, but this idea was dropped under an agreement with the Eastern Counties that gave the Lynn & Ely running powers over the Wisbech, St Ives & Cambridge Junction line. This arrangement thus provided access to the former's Ely & Huntingdon enterprise at St Ives, which was the residue of a planned link to Bedford and the London & Birmingham Railway, just as the Spalding extension had

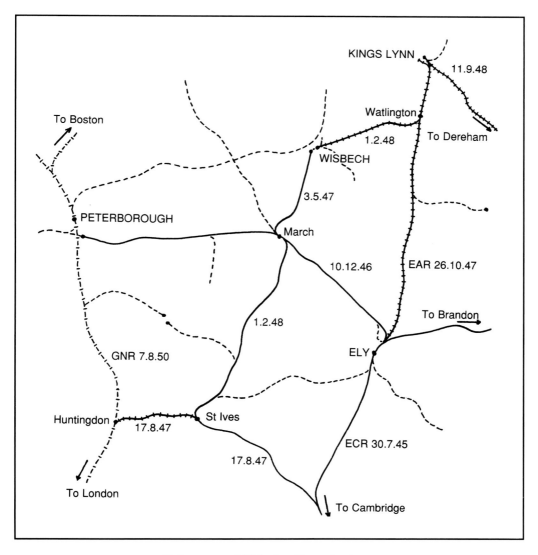

Railways around Wisbech, with opening dates.

been part of a grand plan for reaching Manchester!

In addition to the Lynn & Ely the other two constituents of the East Anglian Railway also obtained their Acts in 1845, the Lynn & Dereham being intended to join up with the Norfolk Railway, which reached Dereham from Norwich and Wymondham on 3 July 1845. The 4 m 55 ch of the E&H between Godmanchester and St Ives was opened on 17 August 1847, when the ECR reached the latter point from Cambridge; the Lynn to Ely line was next into use on 26 October 1847, and the branch from Watlington reached Wisbech on 1 February 1848. The latter was straight and flat but required bridges over the Ouse, the Middle Level Drain and the Wisbech Canal, the requirements of the water authorities proving quite onerous and the soft ground on either side of the canal causing considerable engineering problems.

Wisbech's new railway used a wooden station about half a mile from that of the Eastern Counties, on a site later occupied by Wisbech East. The day of its opening coincided with that of the ECR's March-St Ives section. That company also built a link between the two lines in Wisbech so that by the time the Dereham

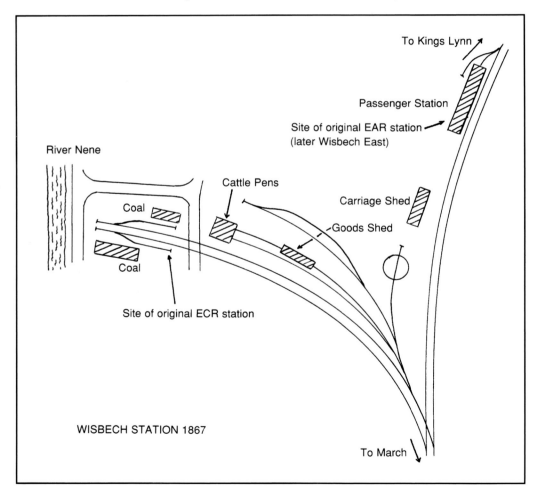

Wisbech's railways in 1867, showing the sites of the two original stations, from a map in the Wisbech and Fenland Museum.

line was completed on 11 September 1848 the East Anglian system seemed both well-placed and well-connected, with lines radiating from Lynn to Dereham and Ely/Wisbech, and running powers from Wisbech to the St Ives-Godmanchester section.

In fact, the situation was much less satisfactory than it appeared. Early negotiations for amalgamation between the East Anglian and its ECR neighbour had foundered, hopes of a Spalding link with the Ambergate company's eastward extension from Nottingham had been abandoned and, due mainly to the high costs of purchasing land and of crossing waterways and boggy ground, the authorised capital of £764,000 had been overspent by half a million pounds. A committee reporting on the East Anglian's problems recommended wholesale economies including the closure of some stations and providing beds at stations for porters in order to save the expense of night watchmen!

The Wisbech branch typified the problems. It had cost more than double the amount estimated, but in adopting a straight route that would serve through traffic, passed too far from the intermediate villages to attract their business. The position was not helped by poor approach roads and, although the service rarely exceeded three daily trains each way, there were many occasions when these ran empty. In the second half of 1848 the company had earned only £18,330 and, despite the implementation of economies, 1849 was to be even worse.

The East Anglian worked hard to surmount its difficulties, but the general economic climate, one of confusion at home and revolution abroad, pushed its creditors into clamouring for payment of the monies owed to them, £280,000 to the debenture-holders and a similar amount to contractors and other bond-holders. The Eastern Counties was proving less than co-operative over the exchange of traffic and gave notice that it would no longer work the E&H section from 1 October 1849. Still the Lynn company struggled on, but a creditors' application to the Court of Chancery eventually resulted in the appointment of an Official Receiver on 29 June 1850. More legal action followed and

at one period creditors were claiming individual items of rolling-stock and the Sheriff's men were riding with every train.

The Eastern Counties chose this period to renew its offer to lease the whole East Anglian system, but the terms were, unsurprisingly, unattractive. On the rebound, the EAR turned to the Great Northern whose agent, Robert Baxter, anxious to fill the trains that had begun running between London, Peterborough and Grimsby (for Hull) on 7 August 1850, saw great possibilities in securing access to Wisbech, Lynn and on to Dereham and Norwich over the East Anglian metals. Other factors were the physical proximity of the systems at Huntingdon and the fact that the Great Northern held running powers over the ECR between Peterborough and Wisbech, obtained under an agreement of 29 May 1849 under which the GN gave up its own plans for a separate line to Wisbech.

At the beginning of 1851 officers of the Great Northern Railway visited their East Anglian counterparts and were given a tour of the system. Further discussions followed and on 16 May the two companies signed an agreement under which the Great Northern would operate the East Anglian lines for 21 years, maintaining the system and its services and receiving not less than 40 per cent of the receipts. The East Anglian company was required to replace the temporary bridges on the Wisbech branch by permanent ones and to effect a junction with the GNR at Huntingdon. The plan was for the main-line company to work the EAR local services from 25 May and the general traffic from 1 July. With the creditors' committee agreeing to the discharge of the Official Receiver to facilitate the new arrangements, better times seemed to lie ahead for the East Anglian Railway.

In its issues of May 1851 the *Wisbech Advertiser & Local Chronicle* was carrying the timetables of the three railways. The ECR details related to trains from the South Brink station to Cambridge and London, the GNR advertised its services between London, Peterborough, Boston and Hull, and the East Anglian entry listed that company's three

50-minute journeys to Lynn with their onward connections to Swaffham, Dereham and Norwich. Then, in the issue of Friday 4 July, the newspaper announced:

'The GREAT NORTHERN RAIL-WAY COMPANY has, we are informed, made arrangements with the East Anglian Company for working the lines of the latter. It is anticipated that a brisk competition with the Eastern Counties Company, as regards the Lynn and Wisbech traffic, will be the result, the Great Northern having powers to run over the Eastern Counties line from Wisbech to Peterborough.'

The words 'brisk competition' were to prove prophetic and in the next issue, No 73 of 1 August 1851, the newspaper was recording:

'The Rival Railways - as we stated in our last, an arrangement has been made between the Great Northern and the East Anglian Railway Companies, by which the East Anglian Lines will be worked by the Great Northern Company. The latter Company, having, by Act of Parliament, power to run over the Eastern Counties Line between Wisbech and Peterborough, in conformity with the above arrangement, issued a timebill at the commencement of the last month, by which trains were to run between Peterborough and Dereham, via Wisbech and Lynn, commencing July 10th. On the morning of the 10th, on the arrival of the first train from Lynn to Peterborough at the East Anglian station at Wisbech, it was found impracticable for the train to proceed any further in consequence of the Eastern Counties having blocked the line by placing a train of waggons across the junction of the Eastern Counties and East Anglian lines, the points for

The surviving access line to Wisbech goods depot in 1993, with the course of the former connection to Wisbech East passenger station straight ahead.

turning the trains upon the latter line having been taken up in the course of the night. The passengers for Peterborough were therefore transferred by omnibus to the Eastern Counties station, and as timely notice of the obstruction had been sent to Peterborough, in a short time a Great Northern train arrived at the Eastern Counties platform, by which the passengers were conveyed to Peterborough. It appears that the short piece of junction line between the East Anglian station and the Eastern Counties Line is constructed out of the limits of deviation as laid down in the Parliamentary plans, and the right of deviation from one line to the other will most likely become a knotty problem of litigation, unless an amicable arrangement is effected. Passengers for London have now the choice of two lines at the same rates, the Great Northern, as will be seen from the timetable, being somewhat the quicker.'

There seems little doubt that this blatant physical confrontation was premeditated. The Eastern Counties had been formally advised of the GN's intention to exercise its running powers between Peterborough and Wisbech and, since the first train from Wisbech for Peterborough was timed to depart at 7.20 am, the ECR retaliation must have been decided upon some time beforehand. Equally, the GN seemed well prepared for hostilities, with a ready omnibus and a spare train to run to Peterborough. Not that too much blame can be directed towards the Eastern Counties company, for the Great Northern was also threatening its Cambridge traffic and this East Anglian penetration was no lightweight matter. Both routes from Wisbech offered five daily services to and from London, but several of the GN journeys were quicker and it also offered connections to Boston and Hull. The latter must have worried the owners of the steamer *Forager*, which sailed from Wisbech to Hull every Tuesday and returned three days later.

With the ECR unwilling to unblock the junction, the GN had to continue to operate the omnibus link between the two Wisbech stations while the dispute was referred to the Railway Commissioners. They heard the Eastern Counties view that the running powers accorded to the GN did not cover the connecting line between the ECR and EAR systems and, although inclined to favour the course of practicality, the Commissioners declined to order the removal of the obstruction when they discovered that the connection between the two systems had never been formally approved by an Inspecting Officer. So the Great Northern applied to the Court of Chancery, reinforcing its intentions meantime by providing its own accommodation at St Ives and drawing up plans for a separate station at Wisbech.

The extent and seriousness of the Great Northern penetration was shown by its advertising of a London-Norwich service via Peterborough, Wisbech and Lynn, with a timing of 8 hours 55 minutes by the 7 am Parliamentary departure from Maiden Lane and 6 hours 40 minutes by the 9.15 am express. But the company was to prove overconfident when Vice Chancellor Turner rejected the request for an injunction to secure the removal of the Wisbech blockage on the ground that the GNR/EAR arrangement was tantamount to a lease and, as such, required the approval of Parliament.

The response of the Great Northern and East Anglian officers was to draw up a new agreement that provided for the former to purchase the East Anglian's plant for £52,000 to fund the work needed on the line. The remainder of the original deal was to be embodied in a submission to Parliament, seeking confirmation of the Great Northern's operation of the smaller system. But then the East Anglian Railway seemed to lose its nerve. Whether motivated by the fear of an Eastern Counties stranglehold or the lure of better terms is not known, but the EAR representatives now approached the ECR with a draft of their new deal with the GN, no doubt hoping it would produce a better offer from the ECR.

The move backfired. Already under some pressure from the GN board over leases and agreements, Baxter bluntly informed his

EAR contacts that the larger company would not be drawn into an auction and the East Anglian could have its plant back as soon as it paid over the amounts owing! The struggling Lynn company got its lines back on 25 November and its plant a few days later, only to find that life was just as difficult as it had been before the GN liaison began. Hoist on their own petard and with no other salvation at hand, the East Anglian directors had no option but to sue for acquisition by the Eastern Counties, which duly took the smaller railway group into its fold from 1 January 1852.

Wisbech was now back in Eastern Counties territory until, that is, the Peterborough, Wisbech & Sutton Bridge Railway opened for goods on 1 June 1866; but that's another story. In the years since then Wisbech East Station has disappeared completely with its place in Railway Road being taken by the Octavia Hill Centre. The first railway line to arrive survived the longest, with the goods depot off Oldfield Lane dealing with inwards trainloads of freight for distribution by road haulage long after other railway activities in Wisbech had ceased.

In use for bulk freight, the last rail depot at Wisbech was once the site of the original ECR station.

14
THE AMBERGATE HIJACK

While the Great Northern was tackling the round of problems with the Eastern Counties Railway to the east and with the Midland and MS&L companies in the northern part of its territory, yet another conflict was brewing, this time in the East Midlands. The adversary was again the Midland Railway, and the prize on this occasion was a share of the lucrative business of Nottingham and its surrounding area.

The instrument of this further period of strife was the Ambergate, Nottingham & Boston & Eastern Junction Railway. This concern had emerged in 1845 as an amalgam of three schemes that all had similar objectives, ie the construction of a major west-east trunk route that would link the industrial area around Manchester with the East Coast ports. The Ambergate Company, as it came to be known, was united with its principal rival in 1846 and obtained an Act that authorised an eastward extension from the Manchester, Buxton, Matlock & Midlands Junction line at Ambergate. The section on to Nottingham was to be joint with the Midland Railway, with Ambergate metals then continuing on to Grantham, Boston and Spalding.

The Great Northern made some tentative moves towards the Ambergate company in 1846 and 1847, but the latter's early years were more concerned with its canal associations than with the preliminary courtship by the GN and Midland empires. The Nottingham Canal was already suffering seriously from railway competition and offered to

> **Protagonists:**
> Great Northern Railway
> and Midland Railway
>
> **Location:**
> Nottingham station
>
> **Date:**
> 2 August 1852

invest in the new railway on the principle of joining opposition it could not beat. The two concerns had directors in common and the upshot of their negotiations was an offer by the railway to buy the canal and pay for it, either with Ambergate shares or in cash, six months after the opening of the line. A similar deal with the Grantham Canal helped to reduce the opposition to the railway's enabling Act.

Like many a company with big ambitions the Ambergate found that, despite the interest of the larger neighbours and the silencing of the main source of opposition, the reality was very different from the dream. By 1849 it was forced to apply for an extension of the time allowed for construction, and in the same Act abandoned its powers for the route west of Nottingham and east of Grantham. At one stroke of the legislation it had been transformed from a prospective trunk railway into a local connecting line. Another economy was to be achieved by means of an agreement with the Midland to use that compa-

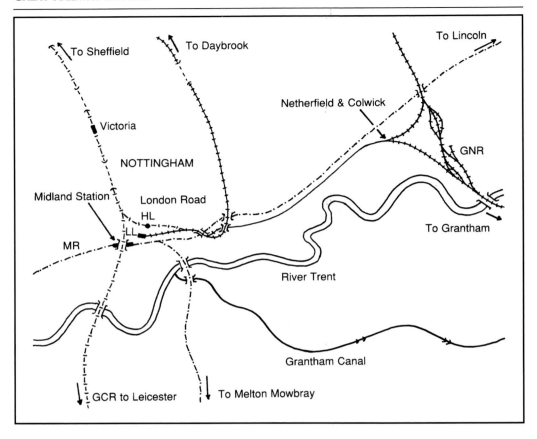

Nottingham railways and the Grantham Canal.

ny's Lincoln-Nottingham metals between Colwick and the Midland station at Nottingham, thus reducing the Ambergate company's construction costs to those for the Grantham-Colwick section. No doubt the Midland saw this as a useful tool for controlling the smaller railway's ambitions.

Eventually the Ambergate works were completed and a double track route opened from the junction at Colwick to a temporary station near the Canal Basin at Grantham. Amid the usual scenes of rejoicing the new railway began operating a service of four trains a day from that point through to the Midland station at Nottingham on 15 July 1850, starting a goods service to and from its Colwick sidings and warehouse a week later. The engine and carriage sheds were at Grantham, but initially they had only two

borrowed passenger locomotives to look after, a new goods engine being involved in a head-on collision soon after its arrival.

Later in 1850, on 7 August, Great Northern trains began running to and from a temporary terminus at Maiden Lane in London and, with the subsequent completion of goods traffic facilities on the Peterborough-London section, the system was ready and hungry for traffic. Coal from the South Yorkshire coalfield was a prime target, with the Great Northern seeking to turn a working agreement made in 1849 with the South Yorkshire Railway into a full takeover. In this it was strenuously opposed by the Midland Railway, which, already in partnership with the LNWR and soon to be discussing amalgamation with that arch-rival of the GNR, was watching every move of the

GN board and its agents. The fact that the advent of the Great Northern had forced the Midland into lowering its rates for South Yorkshire coal did nothing to endear the newcomer to the regime at Derby.

The Great Northern and Midland concerns had already done a little shadow-boxing over the Nottingham traffic. That city lay at the heart of the Midland empire and the nearby coalfield was also too great a prize to be jeopardised lightly. The Midland moved a substantial volume of coal to London via Hampton-in-Arden and the LNWR, and was in no mood to see this siphoned off to an arch-rival. To the Great Northern a Nottingham link to its main line would be an invaluable feeder, and thus both parties took a great interest in any proposals made to build that link.

The interest in the Ambergate line, already quite keen, grew greater as the work on the Great Northern's 'Towns' line from Peterborough to Retford progressed. By an Act of 2 July 1847 the smaller company already had powers to connect the two systems at Grantham and, by exploiting these and the Midland agreement to run into Nottingham station, the Great Northern could see an attractive prospect of obtaining valuable additional business with little or no capital cost. On the other hand, a Midland acquisition of the Ambergate would permit the former to keep its territory intact and to exchange at Grantham traffic on which the full mileage rates could be exacted.

In April 1851 representatives of the LNW and Midland companies met with the Ambergate board and put before them proposals for an agreement under which the MR would work the smaller line at a rental that would start at £2,750 and rise to £6,850 annually. This was no mean offer, and would have helped the struggling Ambergate concern to find some relief from the financial difficulties already arising from modest traffic levels and its commitments to the canal companies. However, after acceptance by the directors, the proposal was rejected by the Ambergate shareholders thanks to the Great Northern's fifth column within the local railway's ranks. This was in the guise of Graham Hutchison, a

GN shareholder of some standing who had also acquired a large holding of Ambergate shares and who used his holding to block the intentions of the Euston partners.

The Great Northern and its rivals came into further conflict during 1851 when competition for passengers to the Great Exhibition was frenetic and fare-cutting a prime weapon. Thus when the GN successfully put its own proposals to the Ambergate company on 31 March 1852, based on a payment equal to 4 per cent on the working capital, the Midland Railway's violent reactions could have been no surprise to anyone. The acceptance of the GN offer, which included a take-over of the canal liabilities, was made by the Ambergate board on 19 May, and immediately the Midland retaliated through the medium of a disaffected GN shareholder, John Simpson. Simpson was also a shareholder in the Grantham Canal, which was still in dispute with the Ambergate over its take-over, and he petitioned in Chancery for an injunction to restrain the Great Northern from working the Ambergate or paying its dividends. The action was successful and the injunction granted on 28 June 1852, the judgement indicating that the payment of a dividend on the capital of another company was outside the intentions of the GN's enabling Act.

With work on the main line between Peterborough and Retford now nearing completion, the Great Northern had no intention of giving up its fight to obtain access to Nottingham, and planned to approach Parliament for an Act of amalgamation with its Ambergate protégé. Meantime close contact was maintained with that company, and although the operating agreement could not commence on 1 July as had been planned, work was put in hand to complete the connection of the two systems at Grantham.

The Peterborough-Retford 'Towns' line was then opened for goods traffic on 15 July and for passenger trains from 1 August. From the Monday, 2 August, Ambergate trains started using the main-line station at Grantham, with the new GNR timetable showing the connections at Grantham for Nottingham and providing a faster service

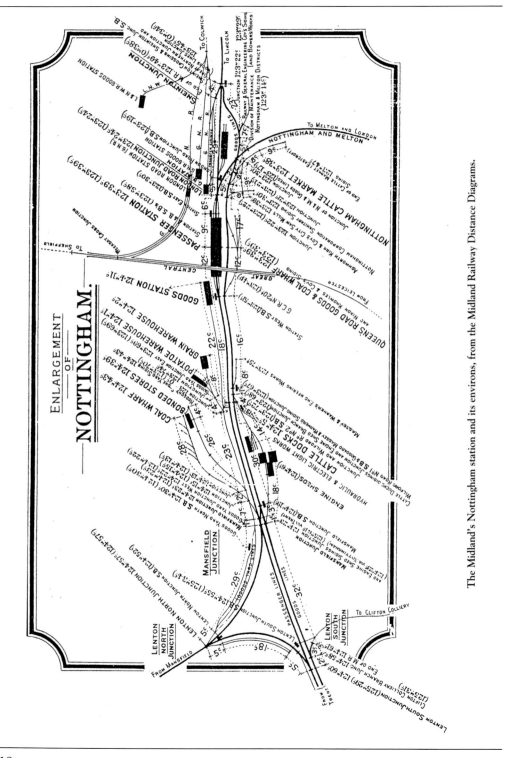

The Midland's Nottingham station and its environs, from the Midland Railway Distance Diagrams.

than the Midland could give via Derby. The latter was now really under threat and the position seems to have been well understood at Nottingham where MR staff had been less than co-operative with those of the Ambergate line ever since the whole quarrel had come into prominence. Tempers were rising to boiling point.

On the first day of the new service there was a deceptive calm until the arrival at Nottingham of the through carriage off the 11 am service from King's Cross. What happened then is described in the issue of the *Nottingham Journal*, which appeared on Friday 6 August:

'During the present week the Great Northern Railway Company have commenced running trains from Nottingham to London via the Ambergate line, the directors of the two railways having recently completed arrangements for that purpose. As the journey by the new route is shorter, speedier and cheaper than the old one, the Midland are threatened with considerable loss of traffic and revenue thereby. This has caused an ill-feeling to spring up between the rival companies and their staffs, which is from time to time displayed in various ways, perhaps the most extra-ordinary of which took place on Monday. In the course of the afternoon of that day a Great Northern engine propelled a down train into the Nottingham station used jointly by the Midland and Ambergate companies and was preparing to depart with an up train, when the Midland Company's engineers placed several locomotives both before and behind it, and took the trespasser prisoner. The passengers had to wait for several hours, until an Ambergate engine could be procured. The Midland Company assert that though the Ambergate engines are entitled to enter the Midland station at Nottingham, the Great Northern engines are not, and that therefore they are entitled to impound the borrowed locomotive as a trespasser.'

Other accounts make it clear that this was not just a piece of local spite, for the instructions to kidnap the GN engine apparently came from Derby and had been given sufficiently in advance for the MR to gather quite a posse of its own locomotives for carrying out the round-up task. The resulting affray must have appeared incredible to those watching. A train from Grantham arrives innocently enough, its passengers detrain and the engine is uncoupled to cross on to one of the two middle roads through the station. Once there it is set upon fore and aft, and although the driver of the borrowed GN engine did try to steam his way out of trouble he was just no match for the power arrayed against him. From other reports the Ambergate's driver seems to have been forced off his engine, which was then dragged in triumph to the out-of-use Midland Counties shed, located between Wilford Road and the old MCR station, and marooned there by the simple expedient of lifting the approach rails. It was to remain so immured for another seven months!

The Great Northern immediately went to court over the incident, relying on the fact that the locomotive detained was legitimately on hire to the Ambergate, was driven by Ambergate men and was the subject of a formal receipt. They lost the action as the Midland/Ambergate access agreement was held to relate only to the latter's rolling-stock and not to that of any third party. The Midland then sought an injunction to confirm the exclusion of GN locomotives and was given the power to certify the fitness of all engines working in from the Ambergate company with the exception of those already in service. There were quiet smiles of satisfaction in the corridors of power at Derby.

The acrimony between the Midland Railway and its Great Northern rival continued in matters practical. Adhering to the strict letter of its agreement with the Ambergate, the Midland instructed its Nottingham staff to accept no goods or parcels for places beyond Grantham proper, so that no revenue should be put in the hands of the GN concern. When the latter instituted its through goods service to

The site of the Ambergate 'kidnap' - the new Nottingham Midland station shortly after opening in 1904, and a present-day view. *Lens of Sutton/Author*

The station frontage, with a new courthouse being built on the site of the old goods depot
and the Midland Counties shed to which the 'hijacked' GN locomotive was towed.

Nottingham on 19 August 1852 the MR denied it access, with the result that Colwick had to be used as the railhead with road cartage to and from that point. On the passenger side, the August York race meeting led to a fares war between the two companies, with each trying to spite the other by undercutting its excursion offers.

Attempting to capitalise on the failure of Midland/LNWR amalgamation plans, the Great Northern itself proposed joining with the former. But the proposal arrived just after a reconciliation between the original partners and rivalry again became the order of the day. A Bill was deposited covering the amalgamation of the GN with its Ambergate partner and for the extension of the latter's line into Nottingham, replacing the Colwick connection with a separate access and station. Although this was rejected by the House of Lords in 1853, that year was made significant on 24 May by an accord that finally ended the Nottingham warfare. Following the thought that the competition was getting costly and ridiculous, the Great

Northern agreed to a pooling agreement, supplementing the earlier 'Six Towns' agreement, under which it would receive 30 per cent of the goods receipts and half of those from passenger traffic. As part of the same negotiated package the GN withdraw its plans for separate access to Bedford and secured additional running powers in the West Riding.

On 3 July 1854 the new Ambergate proposals received the Royal Assent, authorising a line of 2 miles 61 chains from near Carlton Junction, Colwick, to a separate station in Flood Road, later London Road, Nottingham, together with a 61-chain connection to the Midland at Sneinton. The new Nottingham station, called London Road and comprising two platforms plus four lines between, first came into use on 3 October 1857 with final completion of the full range of facilities in March 1858. It was a substantial affair with impressive, chateau-like buildings to house the company's headquarters staff. The payment to the Midland Railway for the use of its station was ended,

Thomas Hine's elaborate headquarters for the former Ambergate Railway at Nottingham London Road Low Level.

although an omnibus link was maintained between the two locations. Other Ambergate changes included new sheds at Grantham, reconstruction at Colwick to match its reduced importance and the removal of the connection to the Midland's line there, and the installation of the electric telegraph along the whole Grantham-Nottingham route.

The 'Ambergate Affair' was now virtually at an end. The Ambergate company itself, which changed its name in 1860 to the Nottingham & Grantham Railway & Canal Co, passed to the Great Northern under a 999-year leasing arrangement operative from 1 August 1861. This provided for a fixed annual rental of $4^{1}/_{8}$ per cent on the Ambergate capital of £1.014 million with a right to purchase outright on repayment of the capital at par. To all intents and purposes the Nottingham line was now a Great Northern branch, although the N&G company did remain in existence until the 1923 Grouping.

Grantham (Old Wharf) was closed to passengers from 2 August 1852 but remained in use for goods traffic, being variously known as Grantham Canal Station or Ambergate Yard. Nottingham (London Road) Low Level lost its passengers from 22 May 1944 and conventional goods traffic on 4 December 1972, but continued to function for a variety of special purposes. The original MCR loco shed has long gone, but the Midland station site of the 'kidnap' remains, albeit rebuilt in 1904.

Today the line from Nottingham to Grantham continues to serve a useful function. As the eastbound trains pull out of the main, ex-Midland station at Nottingham and cross over the canal, the dramatic buildings of the old Low Level station-cum-Ambergate headquarters can be seen on the north side, now starting a new life as a museum. For some 3 miles the old rival routes then use the same metals, but further on the Grantham and Newark lines separate at what was originally the commencement of the Ambergate line. In recent years the whole Colwick area

Netherfield station, formerly Netherfield & Colwick,
with the convergence of the Ambergate and the Midland's Lincoln line ahead.

has been simplified, losing its once notable marshalling yards, and leaving only a spartan island station for train access. At the London end of the main Nottingham station the pre-vious station site now accommodates the new Magistrates Court and Bridewell, bury-ing the former MCR loco depot and its infa-mous kidnap associations for ever.

15
THE GREAT NORTHERN'S SPECIAL SERVICE

The huge traffic potential of Manchester, which had so excited the promoters of the Liverpool & Manchester Railway in the run-up to 1830, was to bring two great railways into conflict in the 1850s. The combatants were the London & North Western Railway, desperate to hold on to its London-Manchester business, and the Great Northern Railway, equally keen to secure a share of it. In the course of their rivalry the two companies were to race their trains, slash their fares, dismay their neighbours and subject passengers to a quite extraordinary level of abuse. *The Times*, in its issue of 4 March 1858, was to say of the conflict:

> 'Here we have two companies representing investments of more than £40 million confided to managers who have neither the intellect nor the dignity to conduct their mutual relations on any better terms than those of a quarter of a century ago when each individual coach proprietor, usually either a publican or a stable keeper, would endeavour to run his rival off the road, satisfied to purchase a drunken triumph at the cost of his creditors and an ultimate appearance in the insolvency court.'

The incidents that prompted this scathing commentary had their origins in the first confrontations between the Great Northern and LNW railways back in the 1850-51 period. The latter's objective then had been to keep the new trunk line out of the North

Protagonists:
Euston Square Confederacy members versus
Great Northern and Manchester, Sheffield & Lincolnshire railways

Location:
Manchester, London Road station

Date:
1856-58

West and West Riding traffic, and it was still prepared to go to any lengths to achieve this. The rivals had seen what competition could do in the period of the 1851 Great Exhibition, when each had been forced to offer fares at a level that often fell below their toll outpayments, and they had been glad enough in August 1851 to accept Gladstone's recommendations for pooling the earnings from six important centres, viz York, Leeds, Wakefield, Sheffield, Doncaster and Lincoln, as a way of solving the problem. But, despite using this to create a pattern for allied fares, the five years of the 'Six Towns' agreement saw a number of developments that put the uneasy alliance under increasing pressure.

The 'Six Towns' agreement and the attitude of its neighbours effectively excluded the Great Northern from the whole of the North West, and limited its West Riding penetration to Leeds and the omnibuses and cartage drays it could work on from there to Bradford and beyond. At the same time the company's superior route and attention to standards of running, comfort and politeness were bringing it passenger numbers that were not adequately recognised in the financial workings of the pooling agreement.

The importance of these factors began to increase with the opening of the GN's 'Towns' line between Peterborough and Retford on 1 August 1852. No longer need north-south passengers make the circuitous journey via Boston and Lincoln, and they responded accordingly, increasing the volume of business through King's Cross and thus putting further pressure on the Euston group. Another such increase came two years later when the GN secured access to Bradford over the Leeds, Bradford & Halifax Junction line, and to Halifax over L&Y metals. Placed at an increasing disadvantage by these changes, the LNWR stepped up its overtures to the Midland and tightened its grip on the impecunious MS&L, concluding a new deal with the latter in 1854. By then, not only was the upstart Great Northern taking much of the West Riding traffic, but Manchester and the areas to the west were also in its sights.

In 1855 discussions about the renewal of the pooling agreements began. The talks now embraced the areas west of Sheffield, but the objectives of the two parties were very different, the Euston group seeking to ratify exclusion of the Great Northern and the latter wanting as much access to the western side of the country as its rivals had to the eastern side. With no concord forthcoming by the end of the year, the LNWR went on the offensive, announcing cheaper and faster services from Yorkshire and Lincolnshire from 1 February 1856. The GN took up the challenge and thousands of people promptly took advantage of the fruits of the rivalry. In five days up to the end of February over 21,000 travelled to King's Cross, but paid only £3,757 in fares.

Later in 1856 an illegal financial agreement between the London & North Western and Midland companies came to light. Challenged

in Chancery the following year, these two partners were now forced to move further apart and end their receipts-sharing deal from 12 May 1857. It is no surprise to find that the Chancery case was brought by a Great Northern director, J. Burkhill, who had acquired £200 worth of LNWR stock on 23 December 1856 for the purpose of his challenge.

Just seven days after the formal end of the LNWR/MR deal the former's general manager, Captain Mark Huish, lacking something in principles but nothing in astuteness, made a remarkable and conciliatory approach to Seymour Clarke, the general manager of the Great Northern Railway. Aware that the GNR and Midland had just come to terms over the latter's use of the line from Hitchin into King's Cross, Huish floated the idea of a new alliance that would recognise some of the Great Northern's ambitions but keep that company out of the LNWR's profitable North West territories. But the remarkable LNWR chief had, for once, miscalculated, as Clarke had no hesitation in disclosing this latest LNW perfidy to Edward Watkin who, knowing the style of his former boss, could see just where such an alliance might leave his none-too-robust MS&L railway.

Prior to 1854 the MS&L had been losing over £1,000 a week and had only survived as a result of its traffic guarantee from the LNWR. This was already running into difficulties, and now Watkin could see the fragile MS&L solvency again in jeopardy if the two main lines were to make their own traffic division. Immediately following the dinner on 1 June 1857 at which Clarke had made new outline proposals to the MS&L, officials of the two companies got together to hammer out details, and by 25 June *The Times* was able to publish the main features of the new alliance, viz:

- full and complete interchange of traffic;

- the two companies to assist one another in every possible way and do everything possible to develop through traffic;

- any additional capital investment to be refunded out of the joint receipts;

- agreement to last for 50 years;

- neither to make agreements with any other company;

- arrangements to be run by a joint committee of directors;

- rates and fares to be agreed and receipts to be divided according to an agreed list of distances; and

- underwriting of MS&L traffic receipts of £10,000 per week.

The boards of both railways considered the new deal on 8 July, the appropriate resolution being carried in both cases. At the MS&L meeting the chairman revealed that the company had received £37,000 from the LNWR since the commencement of the agreement of 29 July 1854, but had routed traffic worth £61,890 via that company in the same period. He also complained about LNW invasion of MS&L territory by means

of the Stockport, Disley and Whaley Bridge line. The LNW response was to point out that it had paid the MS&L significant sums at the beginning of the agreement and complained that it was now being abandoned when things were not going so well. An LNWR report of 18 July concluded that

'. . .there is not the slightest pretence for saying that any sum of money ever was due to the Sheffield company under the agreement other than that actually paid to them. The charges now brought against the London and North Western Company of illiberal conduct in withholding traffic and in deducting 50 per cent on the deficiency are contradicted by the repeated public declarations of the chairman of the Sheffield company.'

The MS&L reply accused the LNW of 'bad faith, attempted unauthorised negotiations for territorial division, a hostile attitude, refusal of arbitration and repudiation of agreements.'

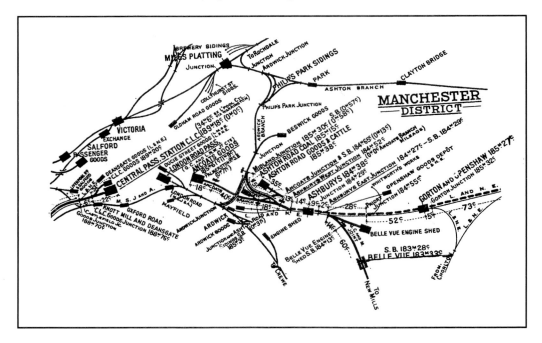

Manchester's railways, from the Midland Railway Distance Diagrams. The trains of the Great Northern's ally, the MS&L, approaching from the east via Gorton, shared London Road station with the LNWR.

Whatever the rights and wrongs of the matter, the truth was that the Great Northern was now in a position to reach Manchester via Retford and the MS&L, and the worst fears of the Euston moguls were about to be realised. At the first meeting of the joint committee of MS&L and GN directors on 9 July a decision was taken to introduce a 'Special Service' of passenger trains between King's Cross and Manchester from the beginning of August. Connections to and from Huddersfield were planned, together with new facilities for goods services and an end to the previous non-co-operation that had made connections between MS&L and GNR trains virtually non-existent (see Chapter 11). With the placing of newspaper advertisements to draw attention to the new developments, the gauntlet had been truly and visibly thrown down.

Meanwhile the LNWR had got in first with a new fast train from Manchester to London. There was no notice to the MS&L, whose chairman said that he was sorry to see looming in the distance 'a course of that sort of petty obstruction which a large company could occasionally practice with regard to a small one, in reference to the occupation of the joint station at Manchester'. This was to prove prophetic.

The 'Special Service' was introduced on Saturday 1 August 1857 with seven GN/MS&L trains competing with ten on the LNW route. The timings of the latter had been improved from $5\frac{1}{2}$ to $4\frac{3}{4}$ hours, and 2nd Class accommodation added to the express trains. The GN required 5 hours 20 minutes for its 202-mile journey, including calls at Hitchin, Peterborough, Grantham, Retford, Sheffield and Penistone, but it was applying its usual high standards and the first up service ran ahead of time all the way and cut 12 minutes off the booked schedule between Hitchin and London. Sturrock engines headed sets of modern Great Northern stock and put up some creditable performances despite the awkward working at Retford where a reversal was necessary after the call at the GN station. The joint committee resolved to build a new curve to improve the Retford position and thus the GN/MS&L schedule.

The LNW could not afford to ignore the GN threat and it responded by carrying the Manchester 'war' into areas other than train running. All traffic formerly routed over MS&L lines was diverted to other routes, and everything possible done to make life uncomfortable for its rival's passengers. At Manchester London Road station the MS&L

Looking west along the former MS&L/GCR route to Sheffield, nowadays burrowing beneath the East Coast Main Line at Retford.

had been glad enough to save a few pounds by letting the LNW operate its portion of the accommodation, subject to three months notice of alteration, but now the Euston company refused to give up control. A sign erected by the GN/MS&L partners was painted over, and the windows of the ticket office boarded up. When the MS&L's clerk managed to force his way in he was unceremoniously ejected, and the atmosphere between the opposing groups became very antagonistic.

Passengers fared no better. Those coming from Sheffield over the MS&L line were bullied and abused, obstructed with barrows, and generally harassed beyond any degree of reason. Other LNW tricks included using a timber train to block the section from Ardwick Junction to London Road, and interfering with the GN/MS&L goods traffic. In one specific case 23 tons of goods that should have been handled by MS&L staff were dealt with by LNW men, and disputes over routing and handling became commonplace.

The King's Cross partners were in no mood to take these actions lying down. They put on extra excursion trains and announced an acceleration from 1 September. By cutting out the Retford stop and taking the curve directly on to the MS&L route, sufficient time was

saved to reduce the through journey to 5 hours which, coupled with the GN standards of comfort and punctuality, was good enough to continue to attract business. With the MS&L unable to do better than 80 minutes for the 40 miles west of Sheffield, the new schedule meant that the GN locomotives had to cover the 162 miles to Sheffield in 220 minutes to maintain the 5-hour timing. Some very smart running was being called for and achieved, with staff along each route urged to contribute to the race and ensure that no delay occurred in their territory.

Once the train timings to and from Manchester had settled into some sort of equilibrium, the emphasis turned to fares and excursions. The Manchester Art Treasures Exhibition had provided the initial lure, but soon hundreds were being carried in response to fares of 17s 6d for a 28-day ticket or 12s 6d for one valid for 3-6 days. Marcus, the LNWR agent, weighed in with an offer of 7s 6d, which the GN/MS&L team then improved to 5 shillings in February 1858. History was repeating itself, and soon thousands were travelling in a fair degree of comfort, at considerably increased speeds and for cheap fares that came nowhere near covering the costs of the train running and other oper-

This section from Ardwick into Manchester London Road station, shared with the MS&L, was on one occasion blocked with a timber train by the LNWR.

ations. In addition to matching the 5-shilling fare, the LNW had increased its original service of eight trains to 11 and cut a further 5 minutes off its best timings.

Meantime the acrimonious competition of this period continued to affect the working at London Road station. A *Times* report of 26 November 1857 describes a situation that developed over the South Junction & Altrincham traffic:

'Yesterday the London & North Western company placed a couple of city policemen at the junction of the South Junction & Altrincham Railway and their own to prevent passengers getting out of the trains of the latter company at the London-road station under pain of prosecution. A lady travelling over the South Junction line to London-road station yesterday morning on alighting to cross the station and change carriages was stopped by these policemen and compelled to give her name and address before she could obtain egress from the South Junction terminus. When she had given her name and address she was informed that she would be prosecuted for trespass. . . About a fortnight ago 200 men removed a platform at the London-road, where passengers from Warrington, Altrincham and other places west of Manchester were set down. They have now formed a siding for empty carriages where it stood and crossing which any passenger is warned that he will be prosecuted for trespass. The claim for doing this is founded on the belief that at the time of construction of the SJ&A line the latter company neglected to get a formal transfer of the land at the point of junction with the LNW.'

A month later another case was reported, but this time the person arrested, a Mr Marsh, was an attorney on his way for an interview with the MS&L general manager. This was different from frightening old ladies, and the LNWR found itself in court when the City of Manchester Police were charged with obstruction and assault. There the assault complained of proved trivial - no more than a hand on the shoulder - and a suspicion remains that the incident was engineered to present the LNW in a bad light.

Another feature of this inter-railway warfare was revealed at the fourth meeting of the GN/MS&L joint committee of directors where a decision was taken to strike further into LNWR territory. From 1854 the MS&L had been able to reach Garston, only 6 miles away from Liverpool, and now trains were to be extended to that point and a service of express omnibuses provided to complete the link with the great city and port on the Mersey. By the use of running powers the partners could also get to Chester, and started to do so, despite a rail removal incident with which the LNWR responded on 1 March 1858. Before long the attack had embraced the Liverpool cattle trade and at a later stage involved links with the steam packet companies that carried the Irish business.

The main period of intense competition at Manchester went on for over 10 months. During that time it extended far beyond the original area of dispute, with the GN/MS&L partners developing their goods and passenger services throughout the North West and the LNW retaliation being felt as far east as Lincoln and Peterborough. The latter's losses alone were calculated by the Board as £75,000, and proved one of the hard commercial considerations that was shortly to bring about the departure of Mark Huish. The public had enjoyed the benefits of fast trains and cheap fares, but the physical violence, obstruction and track-lifting capers, plus unsavoury evidence of the LNW attempting to bribe MS&L staff for traffic information, had all diminished the reputation of the railway industry.

Nor could other railways remain unaffected by the activities of the combatants. Their through business was quarrelled over, their rates and fares jeopardised and, in some cases, their own traffic actually abstracted. Right from the beginning the Midland, L&Y and NER had urged reconciliation, and by March 1858 were arranging meetings to bring pressure to bear on the rivals. Progress was modest at first, an improvement in the LNW rates from Lancashire to Peterborough and then a decision partly to restore the London-Manchester fares and to maintain equality between the two routes. But this was only self-preservation, and a final battle was to still take place in Parliament.

To ratify their position the Great Northern and MS&L companies had presented a Traffic Arrangements Bill. This was to require 25 committee sittings in which the various protagonists protested their sufferings, innocence and ambitions. Even the final sitting took 6 hours before the suspense was lifted and the decision announced in favour of the petitioners. A lesser battle followed in the Lords before the Bill was finally passed on 23 July 1858.

Life slowly returned to near normal. Huish resigned on 11 September and his successor signed an agreement with the King's Cross partnership on 12 November. Effective from the beginning of the following year, it lifted fares to a level 10 per cent below the original

ones and added 15 minutes to the journey times, which allowed the restoration of the Retford stop. The dispute had caused a £28,516 deficiency in the MS&L receipts for the first half of 1858 and brought that company to the point of offering its undertaking to the GN, Midland, L&Y and ELR companies. This was avoided by a GN loan and a payment of £25,000 for a half share in Sheffield station, but the competition had so nearly proved ruinous and the railway map of Great Britain had been irrevocably altered.

Part of the settlement agreement included the enlargement of London Road station and its partition between the two using groups. Progress was slow and the Mayor of Manchester was soon complaining of the lack of action. In fact it was to be 1866 before the alterations were completed. Today London Road is lost in the Piccadilly complex, all London services travel by the ex-LNWR route and only the New Mills/Marple/Glossop services use the former MS&L route via Ardwick Junction.

A DMU pulls away from Ardwick along the remnants of the once proud
- and contentious - MS&L trunk route to Sheffield.

16
BLOCKADE ON THE EXTENSION LINE

In the middle years of the last century even the most forward-looking thinkers had yet to envisage the railway network as extensive as it was ultimately to prove. One major reason was that the population of towns and cities was much lower then, often barely sufficient to provide a good living for one company and certainly not warranting two, especially if they served the same destination area. This situation provided the background to a major confrontation between the London, Brighton & South Coast and South Eastern railways over the Hastings traffic, and lies behind a *Times* report of sentiments expressed by Mr S. Lang at a half-yearly meeting of the Brighton company on 25 July 1851:

'In reference to the Hastings traffic, he did not wish to say one word that would aggravate or throw any difficulty in the way of a settlement with the South Eastern company. The directors of this company certainly did not want to compete for the traffic, neither did he think that the other company wanted to compete for it. He had no wish to blame them for the course they had taken, for the mischief did not rest with them but with the Legislature which had been so foolish as to sanction the construction of two lines to a town for the traffic of which one railway would be sufficient.'

In the 1840s both the South Eastern Railway and the London & Brighton Railway

---

Protagonists:
London, Brighton & South Coast Railway and South Eastern Railway

Location:
Hastings station

Date:
14-26 February 1851 and subsequently

---

expressed interest in serving the town of Hastings, then modest by today's standards but growing steadily and the centre for quite a large area. The former proposed a branch from its main line at Headcorn, while the latter used as its instrument the Brighton, Lewes & Hastings Railway, a company formed with L&B approval and having two L&B directors on its Board. Its Act, which received the Royal Assent on 29 July 1844, authorised not only a double track line from Brighton to Lewes, but also provided for the take-over of the BL&H by its parent and guarantor, the L&B. A further Act, which received the Royal Assent on 8 August of the following year, authorised an extension east along the coast to Hastings, then inland to join the South Eastern at Ashford. To satisfy the ambitions of the latter, the legislation contained clauses to effect the transfer to the SER of the section from Bulverhythe, just west of Hastings, to Ashford, but the Act

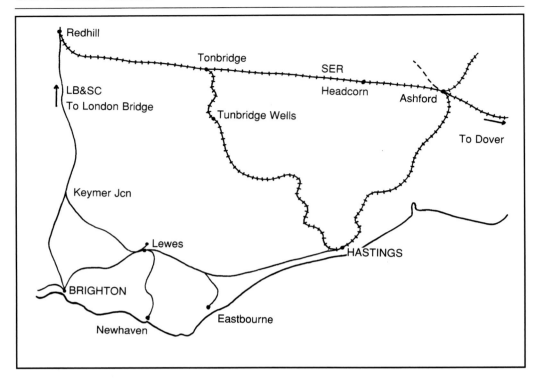

The early LB&SC and SER routes to Hastings.

also provided for the retention of the BL&H running powers into Hastings itself. It also maintained the right of acquisition of the BL&H by the Brighton company.

So far, so good. There seemed no great problems in the situation, but in 1845 the BL&H also received Parliamentary blessing for a cut-off connection between Lewes and Keymer, on the London-Brighton main line, which would produce a direct route from London to Hastings totalling only 76½ miles compared with the South Eastern's 94 miles via Ashford. Then, in 1846, the South Eastern was empowered to extend its Tunbridge Wells line to meet the Lewes-Hastings-Ashford line near Bulverhythe, which would enable it to offer an even better service between Hastings and the capital. Two serious competing routes between London and Hastings were now in prospect, but the town remained modest in size and limited in its traffic potential.

The BL&H line from Brighton to Lewes

opened on 8 June 1846, with a single-line extension to Bulverhythe following on 27 June of that year and the link to Keymer on 1 October 1847. Along with the London & Brighton, the BL&H had now become part of the London, Brighton & South Coast Railway, and under this title was to provide Hastings with its only local railway facility for four years. But work on the SER lines from Ashford and Tunbridge Wells was proceeding steadily and a conflict of interests loomed appreciably nearer. As a curtain-raiser, in August 1850 the LB&SC applied in Chancery to halt the SER work on the Bulverhythe-Hastings section, alleging alterations in the agreed gradients and expressing doubts about safety. The matter was referred to the Railway Commissioners who declined to authorise the alterations, but did not feel that safety was being jeopardised.

Meantime the South Eastern was encountering other difficulties in the shape of the erratic progress of the construction work on the Ashford-Hastings-Bopeep line. In particular, the ground beneath the Hastings approach embankment across Priory Meadows had proved soft and treacherous, with the trackbed level sinking by as much each night as it had been raised by the work of the day. This difficulty was eventually solved by using piles to reach the solid foundation discovered at a depth of 35-40 feet, and by 19 October 1850 it proved possible to run a trial train through from Ashford to Hastings. Thomas Farncomb, Lord Mayor of London and also a native of Hastings, put the final bricks in the tunnels on 28 October, but the line was still bedevilled by landslips and work on the stations was still incomplete.

Thus 1850 ended with the LB&SC operating regular and excursion services to and from Bulverhythe to maximise its carryings while it could. Other passengers travelled by coach to reach the SER main line at Staplehurst and journey forward from there, but all, passengers and railways alike, speculated on a future that would see first a new line opening from Ashford, then the route via Tunbridge Wells that would cut the rail distance to London to 62½ miles.

The reality was to be revealed early in 1851. The South Eastern was then putting the final touches to its line from Ashford to Hastings during January, and the Brighton was ready with the short connection between Bulverhythe and the junction at Bopeep (named after a local hostelry and situated about a mile and a half west of Hastings). The opening date was to be Thursday 13 February, but both parties were on edge. With its previous terminus at Bulverhythe over 2 miles from Hastings proper, the LB&SC was looking forward to getting right into the town. The South Eastern, in contrast, would have preferred to have had the new station to itself in order to offer convenience of access as a compensation for the longer and more roundabout journey to London.

With work finally completed on the last jobs at the stations, completion of the remainder of the tunnel linings and with the several troublesome landslips stabilised, the Ashford-Hastings line was ready for official inspection on Friday 7 February. The inspector's report was considered by the Board of Trade at the beginning of the following week and on the evening of the Wednesday a telegraph message arrived at Hastings confirming

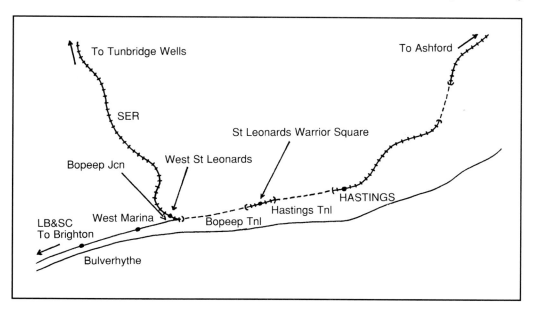

Rail routes in and around Hastings.

The view west from Bopeep along the former LB&SCR line towards West Marina and Bulverhythe.

the approval of the new railway. The good news was quickly passed on to the civic authorities, then spread around the town through the good offices of the town crier.

At 7.15 am on the morning of Thursday 13 February 1851 a small crowd had gathered to watch the first train leave Gensing (now St Leonards Warrior Square) station for Hastings, then on to Ashford. A total of three trains ran in each direction that day, each journey being accompanied by the bells of St Clement's church, which helped to celebrate the happy event.

On the following day, however, the whole situation changed dramatically. The first LB&SC train for Hastings had hardly got started on its journey when the driver was confronted with adverse signals on the approach to Bopeep Tunnel. He whistled for them to be cleared, but without effect, and on enquiry discovered that the order to obstruct his progress had come from Mr Talbot, the SER's station master at Hastings. The latter was on the spot to reinforce his

instruction and, since he showed no sign of changing his mind, the LB&SC engine had no alternative but to set back to its own station.

A heated discussion now took place between the representatives of the two railways. On the South Eastern side were Mr Finnigan, the superintendent of the line, and Mr Talbot, the Hastings station master, with the LB&SC represented by their counterparts, Messrs Hawkins and Sutton. The latter, who was in charge of the LB&SC area at Hastings, was already thoroughly incensed by obstacles placed in his way by his counterpart over access to the LB&SC section of the station offices. The SER officials defended their obstruction of the line by maintaining that they had received no timetable for the Brighton company's operations. Denying this, Hawkins nevertheless provided a further copy and a resumption of normal working was agreed for the following day.

Relying on this agreement the LB&SC distributed wall-posters around the town announcing that a normal service would operate on the Saturday. So it did on that day and the next, but over the weekend a rumour began to circulate in railway circles to the effect that the Brighton trains would be obstructed on the Monday. It was given some substance at midday on Sunday when the South Eastern's secretary, O. S. Herbert, arrived out of the blue and went into immediate consultation with his local officials.

On Sunday night the sinister fruits of their discussions were revealed. Hastings station had been built in a vee configuration with the point westwards towards St Leonards. The northern through platform was designed for use by the SER and the southern one was for Brighton originating and terminating services. By about 10 pm the LB&SC stock in the latter part and its adjacent sidings consisted of seven 1st, six 2nd and two Parliamentary vehicles, plus two luggage vans and two tender locomotives, all worked in

and placed in the right position for working their Monday rosters. All this rolling-stock was then blocked in when an SER engine and a load of ballast wagons was shunted across the access points and left there. At the same time SER workmen removed a 20-foot section of the rails between the LB&SC station and Bopeep tunnel and tipped stone blocks into the gap to complete the obstruction.

Monday 17 February thus dawned with the LB&SC totally unable to operate between Bulverhythe and Hastings. A large portion of its local stock was blocked into the southern sidings at Hastings station and a complete blockage of the line west of Bopeep tunnel prevented any rescue or relief operation. Station master Sutton had found out about the SER's actions at 3.30 that morning and, unable to resolve the operational situation, had concentrated on making sure that the public knew exactly who was to blame. Throughout the town large posters appeared:

The west end of Hastings station looking towards Hastings Tunnel, and with the former LB&SC area, where the company's stock and locomotives were blockaded, on the left.

At the west end of the 1,318-yard Bopeep Tunnel, the signal box and junction are seen from the former LB&SC route from Bulverhythe. On the left behind the signal box is the later 1852 SER line to Tunbridge Wells.

'Notice - In consequence of the Directors of the South Eastern Railway Company having caused an obstruction on the line of rails between Hastings and the St Leonards station of the Company, the trains of this Company will cease to run, as advertised, from the New Station at Hastings, but will run from the original station at St Leonards, until further notice.'

By the afternoon Sutton had gone one step further and procured a four-horse omnibus to work from Hastings to Bopeep, but his opponents were nothing if not determined. Late in the evening the South Eastern retaliated and directed a gang of its labourers to erect a barrier across the station entrance road and secure it with a padlock to deny any road vehicle access. The SER did offer to release the captured stock if the LB&SC would remove it, but Sutton declined, declaring that he was having it valued for legal retaliation!

The following day, the Tuesday, proved no better than its predecessors. By now the SER had a policeman on guard at the barrier, and when the LB&SC omnibus presented itself he promptly denied it admission. Admittedly an enterprising private omnibus was treated the same way, but the constable readily unlocked the barrier for vehicles conveying South Eastern traffic. Sutton entered yet another formal protest only to be told that the South Eastern had no proof that his company was entitled to use the original access powers granted to the Brighton, Lewes & Hastings Railway. The SER maintained that the Brighton company had been reminded of the need to provide this proof two weeks before the new service began.

Although desultory discussions continued throughout the day they failed to break the impasse. The South Eastern showed its resolve by adding a spoil train to the Hastings obstruction and by chaining its wagons to the rails. To thwart any LB&SC retaliation it stationed gangs of men at strategic points, out of sight but ready to rush out if anyone tried to remove the obstructions. This tactic provided a farcical moment when the whistling of an LB&SC engine was taken as the signal for a counter-attack and all the SER 'troops' rushed out of hiding, only to find a Brighton driver whistling for his errant fireman.

On Hastings station itself, Sutton and his small team were virtually under siege. His gas supply had already been cut off and the dull days could be lit only by oil lamps. Now the South Eastern started to saw down the partitions separating the two parts of the station, trapping the LB&SC official in his booking office in the process. 'That gentleman kept to his post, resolved to stand out against the siege, while an inch of ground remained to him,' reported the *Hastings and St Leonards News*.

The ludicrous situation at Hastings lasted until 26 February when the LB&SC obtained an injunction against its rival in a Chancery action. The South Eastern cleared the line that night and normal services resumed. The recriminations were by no means ended, though, and in the columns of the local press a South Eastern report of 1 March 1851 and the subsequent LB&SC response statement presented the following picture:

SE - the LB&SC, without notice, applied to Chancery to stop the Bopeep-Hastings works, alleging gradient alterations.

LB - no alterations should have been considered without previous advice; the LB&SC had repeatedly asked for discussions about lines to Hastings; it withdrew objections to the alterations when the Railway Commissioners declared them safe.

SE - the link to St Leonards was stopped to compel the LB&SC to demonstrate its title to the BH&L right of passage/access; obstruction removed when Chancery so ordered.

LB - title in take-over Act could not be clearer and SER had not queried it during the whole time that the Hastings line was being constructed.

SE - the delay in opening the Ashford-Hastings line was due to waiting for the Railway Commissioners to issue regulations as requested by the Brighton company.

LB - the Railway Commissioners had said that failure to complete the SE works was

Hastings station's modern frontage and forecourt dates from a 1931 remodelling.

the real cause of delay and the additional working regulations referred to had already been discussed and agreed with the SER.

During March 1851 both the London, Brighton & South Coast and South Eastern companies turned their attention away from physical obstruction to competition through services and fares. The level of trains through the Bopeep Tunnel rose to 36 a day and that through the Hastings Tunnel to 51 trains daily. A Brighton fast train left Hastings at 2.20 pm each day followed by a South Eastern express 10 minutes later. From 14 March the LB&SC was operating a 2-hour excursion facility to London and charging fares of about half the normal level.

Like the physical obstruction this sort of behaviour could not last, and from September the two competitors agreed to raise their fares to a more economic level. With the opening of the Tunbridge Wells route on 1 February 1852 a fare-pooling agreement also came into operation and life settled down to a more normal pace at last.

Nowadays Bulverhythe station has long since been forgotten, having closed from 7 November 1846 in favour of Hastings & St Leonards (later St Leonards, West Marina) located nearer Bopeep Junction. At the latter the two lines still merge just before the tunnel portal and pass through St Leonards Warrior Square (originally Gensing) and Hastings Tunnel to arrive at Hastings proper. Hastings station itself was much simplified in 1931 when the old LB&SC area with its two platforms and three stabling sidings largely disappeared under a new building and forecourt area.

17
BETWEEN TWO STOOLS

The branch line to Caterham leaves the Brighton main line via a junction immediately south of Purley station, then runs south-east through the residential districts of a pleasant wooded valley to a modest terminus in the centre of the Surrey township. For many years it has enjoyed a good, half-hourly train service, but few of its regular users could guess at the line's troubled beginnings. These troubles were many and derived directly from the fact that the original line lay in the traffic sphere of one railway company but joined the main line of another.

When the early residents of the Caterham area proposed a railway to open up the district and enhance the value of their properties in the process, they had reckoned without the fragile and suspicious relationship between the emerging railway giants of the counties south of London. And to be fair to those two - the South Eastern Railway and the London & Brighton Railway (subsequently the London, Brighton & South Coast Railway) - the situation was not entirely of their making, but stemmed from Parliament's attempts to restrain the wilder aspirations of the early railway speculators.

The railway network south of London originated with the opening in 1836 of the London & Greenwich Railway, followed in 1839 by that of the London & Croydon line. By then the South Eastern Railway's line to Dover had been sanctioned and a House of Commons committee had recommended a common exit route from London for both the

Protagonists:
South Eastern Railway,
London, Brighton & South Coast
Railway and Caterham Railway

Location:
East Croydon and the
Caterham branch

Date:
1854-62

Dover and Brighton lines. The outcome of this was to be a shared line between Croydon and Redhill, with the section north of Coulsdon in the hands of the London & Brighton and the southern portion with the South Eastern, each to operate toll-free over the other's metals. By 21 September 1841 the L&B was running trains to Brighton and on 26 May 1842 the SER opened to Tonbridge, the latter pooling locomotives and stock with the London & Croydon in 1842 and the L&B joining the scheme two years later.

The pooling scheme ended in 1846, the year that the London & Croydon joined with the London & Brighton to become the LB&SC. With the South Eastern absorbing the London & Greenwich the cross-charging of tolls for trains running over one another's sections could have become complex, but the two growing railway groups were able to devise an agreement to regulate their relationships and define their spheres of influ-

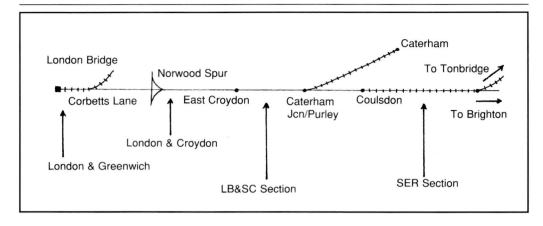

The main line from London Bridge to Redhill/Reigate, showing how it was divided
between the two principal companies.

ence. Heads of agreement had been thrashed out by 12 November 1847, were given legal status on 10 July 1848 and, effectively, gave each partner the right to tolls from the other only on traffic to or from lines that penetrated its home territory. For the South Eastern this was the area north and east of a line from London to Reigate, then to Tonbridge and Hastings, and for the LB&SC south of the Reading, Guildford & Reigate line and west of that from Reigate to Brighton.

On to this cosily divided scene then came the innocents of Caterham, no doubt believing, as many early promoters did, that their line could ultimately be sold to a bigger neighbour at a significant profit. They reckoned without the fact that the proposal lay in South Eastern territory, but would make connection with the LB&SC portion of the main line. When they contacted the LB&SC in 1853 it prompted that company to write to the South Eastern on 21 October as follows:

'The Directors of this Company have been applied to by the parties promoting a branch Railway from Godstone Road Station to Caterham, to give their assent to that line. Under the existing amicable relations with your Company, my Directors do not wish to take any step with regard to the line in question without consulting your Board. . .

I shall be glad, therefore, to hear from you whether your Board have any feeling on the subject.'

The SER reply of 27 October said that the company had no objection to any LB&SC action as long as the traffic was counted as South Eastern with an allowance to the LB&SC for the journey along the main line. Unable to swallow this, the Brighton company sent a two-sentence response confirming its withdrawal from any arrangement with the local company.

The Caterham Railway Act received the Royal Assent on 16 June 1854, a year in which the two main-line companies reaffirmed their mutual intention not to make agreements with third parties in one another's territory. By the beginning of 1855 the Caterham people had signed a construction contract, and were able to hold a small ceremony to mark the cutting of the first sod on 5 March. Another contract was let later that year, and before it was out plans had been drawn up for quarry extensions, which, it was hoped, would yield valuable business. The General Meeting of the Caterham Railway Company on 2 July 1855 revealed that financial and operational proposals had been put to the South Eastern Railway, and a resolution had been adopted empowering the directors to conclude a working arrangement with either that company or Thomas Jackson, the contractor.

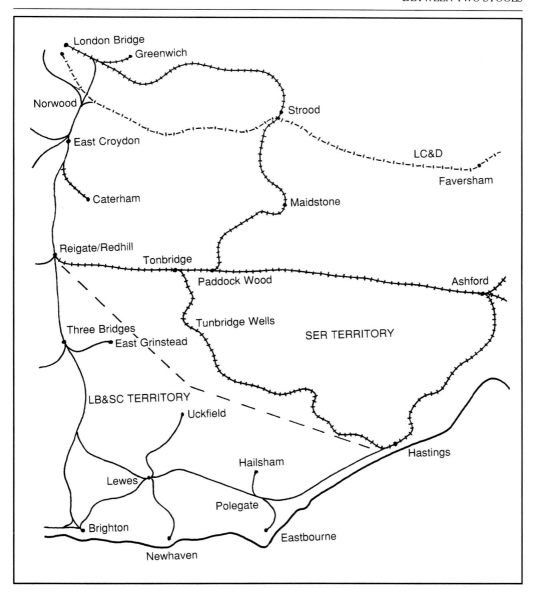

The principal lines in the LB&SC and SER 'spheres of influence', showing the dividing line.

Godstone Road, the LB&SC station where Purley now stands, was one of the early railway closures, having been abandoned at the end of September 1847. And the main-line company showed a marked reluctance to re-open it, suggesting that it was unsafe, then that the Caterham Company should extend to Wallington to join the Epsom line, and finally insisting on a bridge there that would add £2,006 to the Caterham's costs. Other difficulties arose, too. The South Eastern declined to hire out a locomotive and carriages to work the nearly completed branch line, avowing that it had none to spare, and the Brighton proved equally unhelpful. No doubt each of

141

The 15.21 service from Caterham approaches Purley, originally Godstone Road then Caterham Junction, in 1993.

the bigger companies had one eye on the 1847 agreement and the other on each other.

Eventually the Caterham Railway was ready for opening and Monday 4 August 1856 was fixed for the formal proceedings. The event was reported by *The Times* on the following day, when the public could also travel on the railway:

'This railway, which forms a branch line from the old Godstone Road station of the Brighton Railway to Caterham, was formally opened yesterday for public traffic. A special train conveying the directors and their friends left the London Bridge station at a quarter past twelve o'clock and arrived at Caterham about one o'clock. The new line is a single one about 4³/₈ miles in length and passes along the valley of Caterham at a short distance from the common road and terminates, for the present, at Caterham. On arriv-

ing at Caterham the train was loudly cheered by a large number of persons. The company then left the carriages and proceeded over the beautiful hilly country to the stone quarries which are situated about 1¹/₂ miles from the present terminus of the railway. It is intended to extend the line to the quarries by means of tramways. . .

At present there are not many residences on the line and the Brighton and South Eastern railways are to supply two trains each of four each way per day. They are also to grant season tickets to the residents on the line at a cheap rate for ten years with a view to encouraging building on the railway. The line has been constructed by the landowners and other parties in the district with a view to benefit their property. The works are light and the line is in excellent condition. The event was celebrated at Caterham by an excellent dinner furnished by the proprietors of the London Tavern at which Mr Fuller, the chairman of the company, presided. Various loyal and other toasts were given and responded to and the proceedings concluded in a satisfactory manner.'

The local newspaper, the newly launched *Croydon Chronicle & East Surrey Advertiser*, reported the opening later but less prosaically. Apparently the welcoming party included a 20-stone Mr Smith who worked assiduously

to create a convivial atmosphere. He was helped by the farsightedness of the organisers who had arranged the tour of the locality 'with enjoyment by sojourns at occasional halting places where, by careful forethought, champagne and other agreeables had been provided.'

The Caterham Railway's half-yearly meeting later in August recorded that the line had been completed 'at a cost of £37,367, within £632 of capital'. But the directors went on to describe the temporary working

Caterham Railway Station.

Caterham station past and present. The earlier view shows the pleasant leafy surroundings and the Station Hotel opposite; while the more recent one shows that the original building still survives, though much simplified. *Lens of Sutton/Author*

143

The pre-Grouping view shows Caterham with a 4-4-0 tender locomotive on a long train of four-wheeled stock, while in 1993 the platform is occupied by empty EMU stock. *Lens of Sutton/Author*

A short down train of mixed stock behind a diminutive tank locomotive works into the SECR terminus at Caterham, controlled by a small signal box on the up side. Today the valley is still wooded, though the station is much rationalised. *Lens of Sutton/Author*

arrangements with the SER and LB&SC as 'undoubtedly inconvenient to the public and injurious to the proprietors'. They had 'no reason to believe that the railway will not be profitable if they are allowed to charge the same fares between Caterham and London which the Brighton and South Eastern companies now charge in the immediate vicinity, but if those companies are permitted to supply only a few trains per day to the Caterham Junction and to charge the present high rates the Caterham district will, comparatively speaking, be closed.' The chairman went on to bemoan the money wasted on survey and Parliamentary costs in connection with the northward extension originally favoured by the LB&SC and to reiterate their need for 'that accommodation in trains which it was right that they should give them'.

Already one feels sorry for the directors of the Caterham Railway. They had experienced more obstruction than assistance in launching their railway enterprise, and inviting representatives of both of their larger neighbours to the opening event failed to produce any change of attitude. Their line was open but the equipment it used was on grudging loan and the trains that stopped at Caterham Junction, as the reopened Godstone Road was now called, made but poor connection with the branch services. Added to this there was no shelter for those unfortunate travellers forced into long waits and, although the main-line companies had made concessions on season ticket rates, the ordinary through fares from Caterham were comparatively high because of the main-line element that the branch company was forced to include.

Things were so bad that within a few months of the opening the Caterham Railway was ventilating its grievances in the Court of Common Pleas, calling upon its two oppressors to show good reason why an injunction should not be issued in the matters of fares discrimination and the lack of facilities at the junction station. The hearing also revealed that neither the LB&SC nor the SER was offering 3rd Class fares to the Caterham line, but despite this the court would only make a ruling in the matter of shelter at the junction.

The nightmare of the Caterham Railway proprietors was to worsen. At the Traffic Committee meeting of the SE and LB&SC companies on 18 March 1857 they recorded an agreement under which the SER kept the receipts from its East Croydon bookings to the Caterham line and the LB&SC all receipts from Caterham Junction traffic, subject to an allowance of 15 per cent to the South Eastern when such traffic passed in its trains. The minutes also reveal that the Caterham had offered its line to the Brighton company for £23,700, Mr Schuster for the latter stating that 'the present offer was not such a one as he was prepared to listen to, although he might consent to a purchase at a more moderate sum.'

Apparently the LB&SC made a counter-offer of £16,000 for the Caterham Railway but, at about the same time, the SER board was recording 'that this Board had not contemplated the probability of the Brighton Company purchasing the Caterham Line, and they should regard such purchase on the part of the Brighton Company as an infringement of the Agreement between the two Companies. . .' Backwards and forwards went the letters in the middle of 1857 until the South Eastern, with more hope than expectation, suggested 'that in the event of our completing the purchase of the Caterham Line, you should agree to our working the traffic to and from the district free of the Croydon toll . . .' Now it was the turn of the Brighton to reiterate its wish to protect the main agreement by avoiding any such variation as the SER was suggesting!

In the last (Brighton) letter of this series came a paragraph that revealed just how bad the troubles of the Caterham Railway were. It read:

'The Directors desire me further to state, that their applications to the Caterham Company for payment of the amount due to this Company for hire of plant, mileage share of traffic &c., having been attended with no result, this Company will be under the necessity of withdrawing its plant from the Caterham line on the 1st of January next.'

The Caterham Railway had been struggling on during 1857 and had managed to keep its hired services running, despite earlier threats, by making occasional payments to the Brighton Company. But the receipts it was taking met only half the costs incurred in running the service, and still neither of the big companies would consent to purchase even at the £16,000 figure, which itself was less than half of the original construction cost. The year ended with this final threat of withdrawal of the branch locomotive and rolling-stock, and while this difficulty was patched up by a short-term agreement between the parties involved, 1858 was to prove no better than its predecessor for the branch line. It saw the Brighton threatening to close Caterham Junction and an action against the Caterham that resulted in an unpaid debenture-holder being appointed as Receiver.

On the wider scene relations between the South Eastern and LB&SC companies continued to see-saw. Fears of an east-west link from the Mid-Kent company, the temporary permission for SER trains to stop at Caterham Junction, dispute and settlement over the West End & Crystal Palace Railway and again over a spur at Norwood kept the two companies corresponding throughout the 1857-59 period. Slowly, however, agreement emerged for a solution of the Caterham problem based on a take-over of the branch by the South Eastern in return for the withdrawal of its objections to the Norwood Spur, which the LB&SC needed for access to the WE&CP eastwards.

Eventually, by an Act of 21 July 1859, the Caterham Railway passed to the South Eastern for a paltry £15,200 after some last-minute negotiations had resulted in the final withdrawal of LB&SC objections. But while this ended the agony of the branch line's proprietors, it was not the last of the sufferings of its passengers. The peace was to be shattered again in 1862 when the LB&SC extended its

facilities at East Croydon with separate accommodation for the London traffic that was not available to the South Eastern. Advancing six cogent reasons why the latter was not an equal partner in the London-Croydon business - after all, the original London & Croydon company had become part of the LB&SC - the Brighton company reduced its fares and started enforcing all sorts of other restrictions.

A Caterham line user who became a victim of this ongoing strife expressed himself in no uncertain terms in *The Times* on 4 October 1862, beginning his complaint:

'I believe it is a matter of notoriety that the Brighton and South Eastern railway companies, being unable to agree with each other, have long put the patient British public to the utmost possible inconvenience to gratify their private quarrels. It is time that their power of doing so should be curtailed. . .'

East Croydon, cause of further friction between the SER and LB&SCR in 1862.
The 14.18 Bedford-Brighton service departs in August 1993.

The Times itself was behind him and added:

'The art of ingeniously tormenting, which in past days was considered exclusively a domestic study, is now cultivated with eminent success by the managing authorities of British Railways. . .'

The incident that had prompted these strong sentiments had occurred during the previous week when the traveller, a Lindfield man who used the pseudonym Viator Vindex for his letter to *The Times*, set out from Haywards Heath on the 9.5 am up train. This was booked to stop at Caterham Junction, but he could find no data on connecting trains in the various guides to railway services and had to assume that some sort of connection would be available to take him on to Caterham town. This assumption proved optimistic, for he arrived at the junction to find that the connection had left 3 minutes before and he could either wait 4 hours or walk the 6 miles instead! Choosing the latter course and hurrying through his business, 'VV' was back at Caterham station in time to catch the midday up train. He asked for a ticket back to Haywards Heath but could only get one as far as the junction.

Back at Caterham Junction 'VV' discovered to his horror that there was no connection forward for 5 hours this time, and hit upon the idea of travelling in the up direction to Croydon to improve his prospects.

'You must wait till 3 o'clock, sir,' said the porter.

'What?' said 'VV'. 'Are all these Caterham passengers kept here for 3 hours?'

'Oh no, sir. They are going on in 20 minutes, but you cannot go by that train. We are not allowed to book by it from this station and they have through tickets from Caterham.'

This was too much for 'VV' who made it clear that he intended to travel by the next up train whatever the LB&SC's domestic regulations. When it arrived he opened a door and made to enter, only to be seized from behind by the station master and one of his staff. Of rather stout proportions, 'VV' won the tug-of-war to the cheering of the onlookers and the chagrin of the railwaymen. Indeed, the station master travelled with his victim through to Croydon where 'other officials threatened him with the direst consequences'. An offer to pay the fare was refused and the matter ended with the recording of the man's name and address and the threat of prosecution.

More letters followed, all revealing the sorry effect on passengers of the dispute and controls operating between the two railways. Eventually improvements were made and the public annoyance subsided, but not before one final, graphic epistle had appeared in *The Times* of 8 October:

'. . .sent my groom with my horse to meet me at Croydon station. When at Croydon I missed my pocket handkerchief, and before I found it and could pass some lady's crinoline, no other passenger getting out, the train was in motion as I called with my head out of the door. This certainly created a laugh at seeing me in my hunting toggery carried away. At Caterham Junction I got out and a train came up at the moment. I rushed to a carriage and was getting in when the Station Master of the Brighton line pulled me back saying that in addition to the fare that I had paid to Croydon one was due to the South Eastern line and that, moreover, he was not allowed to let passengers get in that train. I paid a trifling extra fare and had to wait until the next Brighton train came up, in the meantime telegraphing to Croydon to detain my horse. Now, perhaps, as some of your proprietors may be hunting men, they and others will be able to appreciate the annoyance to

An Old Foxhunter.'

18
THE BATTLE OF HAVANT

Despite its size and importance, and despite a lot of early discussion, Portsmouth was late in joining the railway network. The reasons lay in its island setting, the inland barrier represented by Portsdown Hill and the prima donna attitudes of the naval and military authorities. The result was that neighbouring Southampton was enjoying services on the main line of the London & Southampton Railway over a year before Portsmouth got any form of railway communication at all. And even when this did come it was only in the form of a branch line from Eastleigh (then Bishopstoke) to Gosport, with Portsmouth travellers still having to get down to Gosport Hard and cross on the Floating Bridge to Portsmouth proper.

When the Gosport branch was authorised on 4 June 1839 the London & Southampton had been astute enough to change its name to the London & South Western Railway, but this sop to Portsmouth sensibilities was no compensation for its branch-line status. The line to Gosport was opened on 29 November 1841, but then closed four days later because of doubts over the safety of a tunnel at Fareham and did not then come into regular service until 7 February 1842. As a route to London it left much to be desired, the crossing to Gosport and 89½-mile journey taking a lot longer than journeys from Southampton or Brighton, which by now also had a direct route to the metropolis.

The trade and shipping interests in Portsmouth were soon voicing their discon-

Protagonists:
London & South Western Railway and London, Brighton & South Coast Railway

Location:
Junction east of Havant station

Date:
28 December 1858 and subsequently

tent, and to add to the LSWR's problems the London & Brighton, which had opened to Shoreham on 12 May 1840, was already planning to continue its westward coastal progression. In these two factors reposed the elements that were to bring the two concerns into head-on collision in a few years time. Meantime their tactics were to promote schemes to secure geographical and tactical advantages over one another.

In 1844 a branch from the LSWR main line at Woking to Guildford was authorised, this being opened and acquired by the larger company in the following year. The LSW company proposed to extend this via Godalming, Haslemere and Midhurst to Chichester and to revive an earlier plan for an extension from Fareham, through Cosham and into Portsmouth from the west. The Chichester extension was designed to meet the L&B-inspired Brighton & Chichester Railway, which would ultimately give the

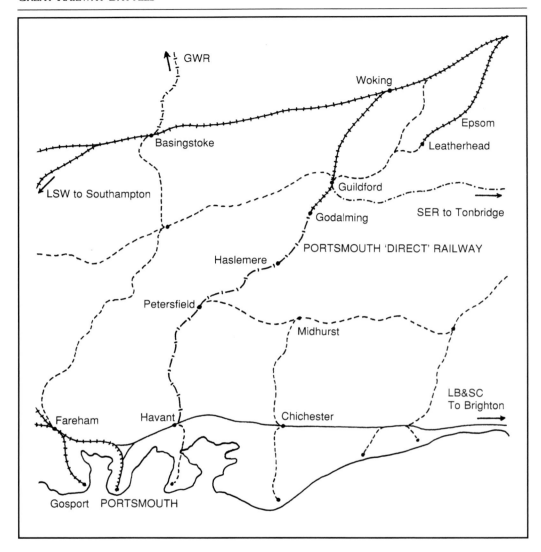

The Portsmouth 'Direct' Railway and adjacent lines.

Brighton company access to Portsmouth from the east. In addition to these two coastal approaches there were 1844 schemes for a Direct London & Portsmouth Railway running from Epsom via Dorking and Godalming and supported by the London & Croydon Railway, and for a totally independent line that had first been mooted in 1838.

In 1845 the Railway Commissioners advised Parliament of their support for the LSWR plans and, after the withdrawal of the independent scheme, the three remaining proposals got through the Commons and went on to the Lords where only the Brighton & Chichester (Portsmouth Extension) survived to receive the Royal Assent on 8 August 1845. This prompted an agreement between the LSW and L&B companies under which the Portsmouth rail approaches from Chichester and Fareham were to become joint property, and they would give their combined backing to the

Guildford, Chichester & Portsmouth scheme in order to shut out the Direct line.

A new twist to the tale occurred in 1846 - the year in which the Brighton's westward progress reached Chichester - with the amalgamation of the Brighton and Croydon companies as the London, Brighton & South Coast Railway. The latter now supported the Direct scheme, and in a further approach to Parliament that and the backing of Portsmouth town led to its authorisation on 26 June. The consolation prize for the LSWR was authority on 27 July 1846 for a connection from Guildford to the Direct route at Godalming, and for a line from Fareham via a junction with the Direct at Cosham and on to the LB&SC's station at Portsmouth.

This intriguing balance of power, mostly in the LB&SC's favour, came to nothing because of the deteriorating financial climate. The Brighton & Chichester, now in the hands of the LB&SC, did reach Havant on 15 March 1847 with extension to Commercial Road, Portsmouth, on 14 June, but work was not even started on the Direct scheme. Furthermore, the LSW and LB&SC companies saw the wisdom of settling their differences and came to an agreement for pooling the receipts from the Portsmouth traffic. The former opened a line from Fareham to Cosham on 1 September 1848, then on to the LB&SC at Portcreek Junction, its first train reaching Portsmouth on 1 October over the Cosham-Portsmouth section, which, under the new accord, became jointly owned. The friendly relationship between the two main-line companies even planned joint ownership of the Direct route, but once the economy picked up again old rivalries were to put an end to the cosy agreement for sharing the Portsmouth business between the two circuitous coastal routes.

The arrangements for a joint approach line and terminal at Portsmouth, derived from an Act of 1847 and embodied in an agreement of 9 October 1848, were updated in August 1852 when the Gosport traffic was also embraced in the receipts pooling and division. However, in the same year the two major railways were confronted by a revival of the Direct scheme, this time involving a route from Godalming through Haslemere to Havant. Railway contractor Thomas Brassey figured prominently in the new challenge, which received the support of the townsfolk of Portsmouth at a public meeting in December 1852.

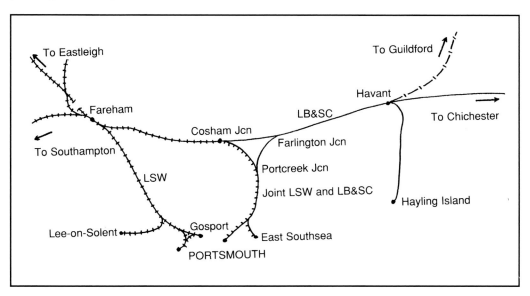

Railways in the Portsmouth area.

The new Direct railway went on to secure its Act on 8 July 1853 and in the following year took over some of the assets of the original company when that was wound up. Needless to say, the established railways were not greatly pleased to see a potentially serious rival prosper, and entered into an agreement 'not to afford any facility to the new and competing railway'. At a later date the LB&SC was to allege that the LSW had actually encouraged Brassey to back the revival of the Direct line, which could have little prospect of a long-term independent future and was clearly built to be sold to the highest bidder.

Brassey, appointed contractor to the new railway, had already built speculative railways in anticipation of their ultimate purchase by an existing railway. After the cutting of the first sod on 6 August 1853 he pushed ahead with the work and in 1854 secured an Act for a connection with the South Eastern Railway at Shalford which would give the Direct line a link to London Bridge. However, the SER declined an informal proposal to take over the embryo railway.

For reasons of economy the new line was built as a single track with quite severe curves and gradients. It also involved extensive excavation, mainly for Buriton Tunnel and the earthworks at Haslemere and Whitley, but by the end of 1857 completion was near. The new company had made no provision for purchasing locomotives and rolling-stock, another clear signal to the LB&SC and LSW companies that it would be looking for a purchaser. But the offer of the line to the LSW for 45 per cent of the gross receipts was rejected, and talks with the SER over access to London Bridge and with the LB&SC over using its line from Havant to Portsmouth all came to nothing.

1858 was a complicated year. In January the LSW and LB&SC companies signed a new traffic agreement, and for six months neither would disrupt the status quo. Then, on 12 July, the Portsmouth Railway got a further Act that authorised its own line from Havant to Hilsea and Cosham, running powers over the Portsmouth access lines and an independent Portsmouth station if agreement could not be reached for accommodation at the existing one. Quite apart from its agreement with the LB&SC, the LSW had been hesitating about leasing the Direct line because its fares would be 25 per cent less than those applying on the existing Portsmouth-London route, and the probable earnings, when taken together with lease costs of £18,000 a year and operating expenses of £20,000, would actually result in a deficit. But after the Direct had survived the sharp contests in both Houses of Parliament and secured this new Act, the South Western now really had no alternative but to come to some agreement with the intruder. At two special meetings the shareholders called upon their directors to take up a lease at the £18,000 figure previously mooted.

The publication of the Bill for the LSW take-over of the Portsmouth Railway provoked an angry reaction from the latter's original Portsmouth supporters. In a petition of protest they complained about the LSW company's clear intention to abandon the favourable fare structure they had been promised and to apply instead the fare levels obtaining on the existing 95-mile route. No doubt the railway saw this as a way out of the unsatisfactory financial dilemma mentioned previously, but Parliament would have none of it and responded by the insertion of protective clauses in the eventual Act and including stipulations covering a minimum train service and a level of speed no less than that applying on the Southampton line.

Whatever the South Western's doubts and difficulties, the balance of advantage had now clearly shifted in its favour and the LB&SC began to signal its apprehension. It rejected the LSW offer of a profit and loss involvement in the Direct line and clearly wanted it treated as 'joint'. A further LSW proposal was based on all traffic, including that on the new route and the Godalming-Woking section, being embraced in the pooling scheme and divided two-thirds (LSW)/one-third (LB&SC) after deductions of 20 per cent for passenger traffic expenses and 25 per cent for goods.

LB&SC counter-proposals were accepted by the LSW as a basis for discussion, but were peremptorily withdrawn when the LSW signed the agreement with the Direct company on 24 December and announced that it would be implemented from 1 January 1859. The December correspondence showed the LB&SC voicing its opposition to the use of the joint station for Direct line trains, the LSW saying that they were going ahead anyway and the Brighton declaring that it would not tolerate Direct line trains over its Chichester Extension. The matter had previously been referred to the arbitration of T. E. Harrison, the chief engineer of the 4-year-old North Eastern Railway, but his decision was a long time coming and the LSW decided that it could wait no longer to start moving traffic over its new route.

Opening of the Direct line to passengers was announced for 1 January 1859, but the LSW planned to run a 'trial' goods service three days earlier and advised the Brighton company to this effect. Frostily, the latter replied that the passage of trains through Havant 'would be opposed until the terms for using the railway from Havant to Portsmouth had been decided upon'. Both companies were now clearly expecting and preparing for trouble, but the LB&SC struck first and during the night of 27/28 December removed the junction points at Havant. For good measure it brought up an old Bury engine and placed it on the up line so as to block any LSW movements.

The LSW's traffic manager, Archibald Scott, also had his plans for a pre-emptive strike. His goods train, with two engines hauling a rake of open wagons, was run 3 hours early and brought a host of labourers, platelayers and railway police to the scene. The contingent, totalling some 80 men in

An early local engraving entitled 'A Bird's Eye View of the London & Portsmouth Direct & the LB&SC Railway Junction, Havant.' The Direct line curves away to the left at the top of the picture, with the LB&SC Chichester line straight ahead.

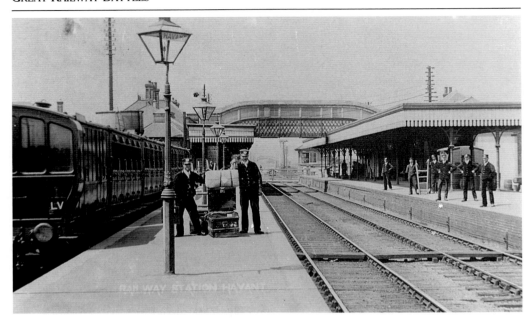

A later pre-Grouping view of Havant station, looking in the same direction. *Lens of Sutton*

all, arrived at the junction at 7 am, only to be halted by a hand signal and the news that further progress was blocked by the missing rail and the stationary Brighton engine.

The Brighton officials were reinforced by their own men who had removed the junction points, and when the South Western contingent alighted the two 'armies' were soon in noisy confrontation. There was lot of jeering, jostling and barracking as the LSW officials threatened the Brighton switchman with being taken into custody unless he restored the missing points section. The man remained adamant in his refusal, so a party of the invaders was sent to hustle the LB&SC enginemen from their footplate and move the engine into a siding. At this point serious violence seemed a real possibility; the two sides had several hundred men in confrontation, the junction was blocked by the South Western goods and this, together with the missing rail section, prevented all normal trains from proceeding.

Still determined to press his right of passage, Scott now ordered his LSW train forward over the up line to the station, where it could cross over to the down. But Hawkins,

his opposite number, had seen this coming and removed another section of rail to the west of the station crossing. By now much of the morning had passed. A crowd had gathered to witness these extraordinary events and the civil police had arrived to make sure that tempers did not boil over. The unfortunate users of the LB&SC line were having to leave their trains at Havant and walk through to Emsworth, empty stock being worked to and from these points to accommodate them. Clearly matters could not go on like this and eventually there was no alternative but for the trial train to retreat. It did so amid cheering from the LB&SC supporters whose own train home was suitably beflagged to celebrate the repulsing of the invaders.

The battle was now transferred to the courts, and the LSWR was forced to operate to and from a temporary station just short of the junction at Havant. From there four-horse omnibus vehicles provided a 25-minute connecting journey to and from Portsmouth proper, the departure time from Nance's Coach Office at Portsmouth being 1 hour before that of the trains from the makeshift station at Havant.

A modern view of the scene of the LSW/LB&SC confrontation;
a four-car EMU passes from the 'Direct' line on to the former LB&SC section.

This footbridge over the former 'Direct' line at Havant marks the approximate site
of the temporary station forced upon the LSWR.

In the Vice Chancellor's court on 19 January 1959 the London, Brighton & South Coast Railway sought an injunction to prevent the LSW and Portsmouth companies from using the station at Landport, Portsmouth, for the booking of passengers travelling on the Direct line. The plaintiffs maintained that the Portsmouth Railway Amendment Act of 1858 might have entitled that concern to use the joint line by agreement, but it did not confer a right to use the joint station. Sir W. P. Wood would have none of that argument and ruled that passengers booked by the LSW were theirs, irrespective of the route by which they might travel. This judgement allowed the LSWR to resume services on the Direct line from 24 January with a 7.15 am from Waterloo getting to Portsmouth at 10.5 am, and a 7.40 am up service reaching London at 10.18 am.

But the LB&SC had not done with the courts and at the beginning of February brought forward two of its employees in actions against London & South Western staff at the scene of the Havant confrontation. Joseph Duckworth, the LB&SC engine driver, charged William Amwell with wilful obstruction, and platelayer John Gates alleged this and common assault against Alexander Ogilvie. Gates gave this account of the events on that dramatic occasion:

'I am a ganger of platelayers on the Brighton line, and was so on the 28th December last. On that morning I was at the Havant station. Between two and three o'clock in the morning I removed, by direction of my superiors, a portion of the line forming the junction with the Brighton and South Coast Railway. The rails belonged to the Brighton company; but were not a portion of the main line. If the rails had not been taken up, a train might have run upon the main line from the Direct railway. About 7 o'clock in the morning I observed a train coming, and showed a red light as a signal of danger. I saw Mr Ogilvie get out of the train (which was coming from Petersfield). The train stopped after I had showed the light. About an hour

and a half afterwards, I was on the Brighton line; during that time the persons in the train put down lines in place of those I had taken up. Finding that the tongue was gone, they backed the train and came up on the other line. I took the tongue up and sent it to Bedhampton. Afterwards I took other rails up according to orders, to prevent the train passing over to the Main line, and locked them up. The engine was on the Brighton line at the time, and obstructing the way about an hour and a half. After the train came up, Ogilvie asked me whether I was ganger of the line. A man pointed to me and said, "That's the ganger". Ogilvie then asked me where the tongue was and I said I didn't know where it was gone. He then took hold of me by the collar, shook me, and said, "If you don't tell me where the tongue is, I'll lock you up". He added it was his property and he had bought and paid for it, and I robbed him.'

The court did decide that the defendant had exceeded his duty and fined him 1 shilling plus costs, but this was such a token punishment that the other case was not proceeded with.

On 25 February the LSW put forward proposals for (a) common rates and no competition, (b) all Portsmouth traffic to be joint and its receipts divided two-thirds/one-third after deducting £15,000 per annum for the rent of the Portsmouth Direct, and (c) an option for the LSW to become joint owners of the Havant-Hilsea section. In its reply on 2 March 1859 the LB&SC proposed arbitration, but this was rejected. With some £35,000 worth of annual business at stake, the Brighton company decided to go to appeal with the legal issues and to take the conflict into the day-to-day operations by abandoning the erstwhile traffic agreement. It instituted a period of intensive fares competition immediately after the LSW Bill for a lease of the Direct line had passed the Commons committee hearing.

During the months that followed both railways competed recklessly for business. The

LB&SC dropped its 3rd Class London fare to 5 shillings return, then started a daily excursion train costing only 4 shillings, and with a journey time down to 2¼ hours. The South Western responded with two fast excursion services daily at a fare of only 3s 6d. The former even provided free steamer services on to the Isle of Wight, and struck at the heart of the LSW empire with a steamer working to and from Southampton!

When the LB&SC appeal resulted in a reserved judgement the LSW was forced to restore its omnibus services for a while, but the competition was proving very expensive for both parties. The Brighton company carried 92,000 more 2nd Class passengers, but took £2,000 less in receipts, while the South Western's increase in passenger revenue proved to be £17,000 less than the rise in working costs! The time had come to call a halt.

On 6 August 1859 the *Hampshire Telegraph* reported that the LB&SC and LSW directors had met and come to terms. The LB&SC was to enjoy one-third of the Direct line benefits for one-third of the £18,000 rental, with a reciprocal payment for the passage between Havant and Hilsea. It was further agreed that the Epsom and Leatherhead line should be joint and that instructions should be issued to agents to end all hostile surveys. The Direct line became part of the LSW company by an Act of the same year, with the rental payment being converted into annuities for the benefit of the independent line's shareholders.

With the renewal of the LSW/LB&SC pooling agreement and the absorption of the 'Direct' Portsmouth Railway by the former, sanity at last returned to the Portsmouth railway scene. Now the signalman looks out from his down-side box at the country end of Havant station on a barrier crossing and an unobstructed junction beyond. Intensively used by trains on both lines, any blockage there would be unthinkable today.

19
A RURAL AFFAIR

Most of the dramas recorded in this book have been played out at busy traffic centres or strategic junctions, but the 'Railway Battle at Bradfield', as the headline of the *Essex Standard and Eastern Counties Advertiser* labelled it, took place on the outskirts of a tiny village in a remote part of rural Essex. Not that the bucolic location in any way detracted from the noise, excitement and belligerence of the event, in which over 100 men fought for the possession of partly completed railway works.

The line involved in this incident was the Mistley, Thorpe & Walton Railway, the brainchild of one Robert Free, a maltster of Mistley, who believed that the Essex coast between Clacton and Walton was ripe for development and would need good rail links with the growing inland network. He was able to persuade local Member of Parliament Captain H. J. W. Jervis to chair the enterprise and enlisted the support of other prominent men in the area, among them a member of the influential Cobbold family that had earlier backed the Eastern Union Railway.

At the time Free was soliciting support for the Mistley, Thorpe & Walton Railway, another company already had plans to penetrate that area of Essex bounded by the Stour estuary to the north and the Colne to the south. This was the Tendring Hundred Railway, incorporated in 1859 and opened from Hythe to Wivenhoe on 8 May 1863. With work on a link to Brightlingsea already in hand, the Tendring Hundred company sought and obtained powers for an extension

> **Protagonists:**
> Mistley, Thorpe & Walton Railway
> and its contractor,
> William Munro
>
> **Location:**
> Bradfield, near Mistley, Essex
>
> **Date:**
> 11 April 1865

from that line to Walton-on-the-Naze to complete a through route between the coast and the Great Eastern Railway's main line at Colchester.

The MT&W scheme aimed to provide an equivalent rail link from Ipswich via Manningtree. Its line was to leave the GER's Harwich branch just beyond Mistley and run through Tendring to Thorpe-le-Soken. From there to Walton the route was similar to the one in the Tendring Hundred plans. Both budding railways had been wise enough to discuss their intentions with the Great Eastern and had received a promise of financial support in return for conforming with the larger company's wishes in relation to track standards and other operational matters. Out of these discussions came an agreement to use a single route for the Thorpe-Walton section, that of the Tendring Hundred Company eventually being chosen.

After depositing its Bill and plans at the end of 1862, the Mistley, Thorpe & Walton

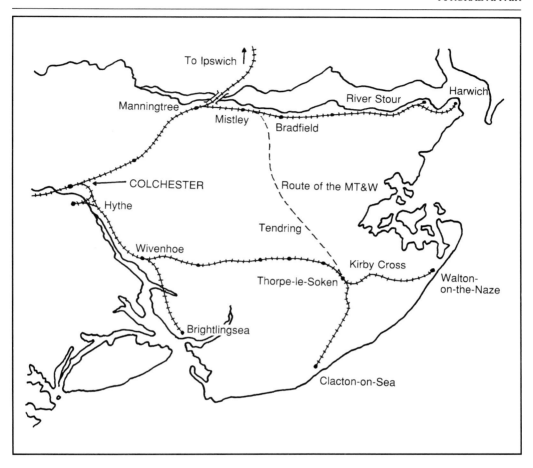

Railways in East Essex.

Railway obtained its incorporating Act on 21 July 1863. The authorised capital was £60,000, and 5 years were allowed for completion. Provision was also made for the line to be worked by the Great Eastern, which would subscribe £20,000, appoint two of the directors and retain 48 per cent of the receipts. By the time the MT&W concern held its first half-yearly meeting at the White Hart at Manningtree on 19 October 1863, the discussions on the use of a common Thorpe-Walton route with the Tendring Hundred Railway had been finalised. Their conclusion was endorsed at the meeting and by a subsequent additional Act, of 30 June 1864, which provided for the 2½-mile connection between the two railways and addi-

tional capital and borrowing powers of £15,000 and £5,000 respectively.

By the time the second half-yearly meeting was held, this time in London on 29 February 1864, sufficient funds had been raised to warrant starting on the physical works. The first sod was cut near Mistley on 6 April at the point where the new railway was to cross the Harwich Road. A special train brought officers and guests from London and they were welcomed by crowds and a band at Mistley station from which they went forward by road in a procession led by a float carrying the ceremonial barrow and silver spade. Speeches made, prayers said and the ceremonial turf removed, the party adjourned to a well-deserved lunch at Robert Free's malt-

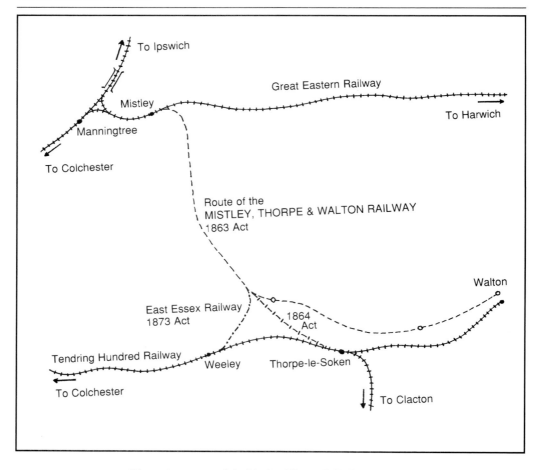

The various routes of the Mistley, Thorpe & Walton Railway.

ings. All this hospitality was paid for by William Munro, the MT&W contractor. At the time Munro was riding on a wave of success, having already obtained other railway construction contracts for the Colne Valley and Brightlingsea lines.

Optimism remained the keynote when the third half-yearly meeting was held back at the White Hart Inn, Manningtree. The *Essex Standard* recorded the directors' report thus:

'In presenting the third half-yearly Report to the Shareholders the Directors have the satisfaction of stating that they have purchased on terms equitable to all parties the land required for the construction of the first section of the line,

viz from Mistley to Tendring. The contractor leads the Directors to believe that he will have the first section of the line. . .completed and ready for traffic by the 1st of June. Arrangements are in progress for obtaining possession of the land forming the second section of the line. An advantageous agreement has been entered into with the Great Eastern Railway Company for the sale to them of the surplus ballast from the cutting on your line of Railway and Works.'

It went on to say:

'The Chairman and Directors, accompanied by the Engineer, &c., afterwards

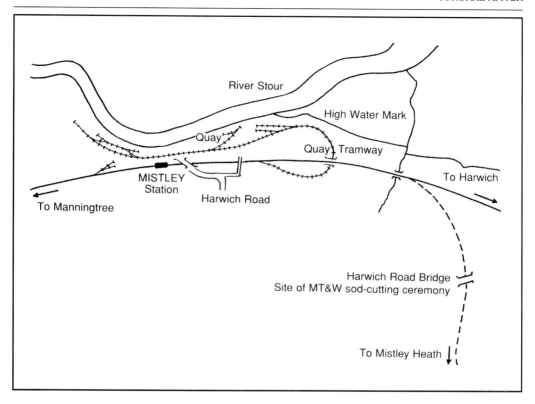

The GER, quay lines and MT&W junction at Mistley.

Mistley station as it is today, looking west.

made an inspection of the railway works in progress between Mistley and Tendring, including the brick bridge, carrying the Harwich Turnpike Road, which is completed with the exception of parapet walls, and two iron girder bridges on the Wix Road. The first passenger station is intended to be at Tendring, near the Union-house - a convenient spot for the Wix and Oakley traffic. The distance from Mistley to Tendring will be about 5$\frac{1}{2}$ miles; and from Tendring to the Junction with the Colchester and Walton line at Thorpe about 2$\frac{3}{4}$ miles.'

The MT&W directors were also encouraged by the success of a tramway opened by the GER from its Harwich branch to the port area at Mistley, the branch showing an increase of £980 in the first three months of 1865.

Despite the optimistic tenor of this report

all was not well with the Mistley, Thorpe & Walton Railway enterprise. Munro, the contractor, was not getting on very fast, partly because of bad weather, difficulties with some farmers and delays in acquiring some of the land, and partly because he had become over-extended by trying to complete the construction work on the Colne Valley and Brightlingsea lines at the same time. Having several contracts, he ended up by satisfying none of his clients.

Whatever the justifications, this situation was quite unacceptable to the Mistley, Thorpe & Walton proprietors and their engineer James S. Cooke. That gentleman made his dissatisfaction known to Munro in no uncertain terms and reallocated his work to another contractor, Frederick Furness. Munro protested, detailing all the difficulties he had encountered, but Cooke was unmoved and even cut one of the contractor's invoices by 90 per cent. The last straw for Munro was when the incoming firm

The line to Harwich as it leaves Mistley today, looking towards the site of the junction planned with the MT&W line.

refused to take over the rails and materials he had paid for.

The *Essex Standard* again takes up the story under the headline:

RAILWAY BATTLE AT BRADFIELD

'. . .Under these circumstances Mr Munro refused to give up possession of the works; and on the other hand Mr Furness, the new contractor, called upon the company to give him the necessary induction to his undertaking. After some unsuccessful parleying it became evident that force alone could affect a dislodgement; and the 11th of April was chosen for the fight.

The late contractor's force consisted of some 50 navvies under the command of the agent, the veteran "General" Fryer, who lately fought so fierce and stern a campaign with a certain Highway Board not a hundred miles from Lavenham; and although the Board remained nominally masters of the field, he at least succeeded in dictating his own terms, as well as his own time, of surrender. On the part of the company some 60 lumpers or long-shore men had been brought up from Harwich, the command of whom was taken by Engineer-General Cooke, assisted by the Solicitors General Cobbold and Owen and Secretary-General Sizer. General Fryer, in order not to be taken in rear, chose the head of a cutting as his position of defence. . .

The position was a somewhat difficult one to turn, and several smart skirmishes were engaged in without any decisive result. At length, however, the company's forces. . .made a rush at and captured General Fryer, while the navvies, with equal determination and apparently equal strength seized him from behind. . .

The view from the bridge seen in the previous photograph, showing the former quay connection at Mistley with the maltings and the River Stour beyond.

And truly the luckless general seemed in imminent peril either of strangulation or dismemberment. Eventually the lumpers prevailed over the navvies, who fled in disorder leaving their General to be "lifted" ignominiously beyond the Company's boundaries. Fryer was not, however, a man to succumb to a first reverse; collecting the scattered remnant of his force he marched on to the next cutting, and there made a second stand; but his navvies were evidently indisposed to come again to close quarters with the sturdy lumpers; and although the General himself disdained to fly he could only offer a passive resistance and the process of "lifting" was again performed upon his person. Still undismayed, he attempted a third stand at another point of the line, but further resistance was evidently useless, and having been once more ousted, the new contractor was installed in possession on the part of his predecessor, and the questions at issue between them, as well as between Mr Munro and the Company, were left to be determined by another tribunal.'

The numbers involved in this affray indicated that it was an affair of some seriousness with real fighting in the first encounter. The longshoremen would be tough, hardy souls, with the navvies every bit as determined, for their jobs were at stake, and it seems likely that little quarter was sought or given. However, when the Harwich group started to gain ground, the 'troops' of the luckless Fryer did not stay to contest the matter again and, apart from a faithful few, Fryer was left to make his gestures of defiance on his own. Brave he may have been, but in the end he must have felt mildly foolish and not a little disenchanted with the lumpers' less than gentle 'lifting'.

Although he had chosen not to make a personal appearance at the 'Battle of Bradfield', the affairs of poor Munro seemed to go from bad to worse. In a supplement dated 13 September 1865 the *Essex Standard* reported a meeting of the Wivenhoe & Brightlingsea Railway that was threatening to take its work away from Munro in consequence of his 'proceeding so very slowly with the works of the line for so long a period'. This time Munro applied to the Court of Chancery for an injunction to prevent the W&B discharging him, but his case was rejected, both by Vice Chancellor Sir John Stewart and on appeal to the Lords Justices. Frederick Furness again took over from Munro who eventually went bankrupt.

By this time the MT&W had secured another Act, on 9 May 1865, which reduced its authorised capital to £36,000, a figure more in line with the reduced mileage to be built to Thorpe-le-Soken. By the time of the next meeting, on 30 August 1865, the outlay of £14,720 reported in February had nearly doubled, and still the line was not ready. Completion of the first section was now expected at the end of November, with the remainder to follow in the spring of 1866. The sum of £12,000 needed to effect completion was to be raised by mortgage. However, despite all the cheery optimism of the directors, including talk of an extension westwards from Manningtree to the Stour Valley at Bures, the signs that the MT&W was running out of steam were becoming increasingly clear.

The Tendring Hundred Railway had also been affected by the difficulties with William Munro, but it was finally opened to Thorpe-le-Soken and Kirby Cross on 28 July 1866, and on to Walton on 17 May 1867. This success seemed to worsen the plight of the Mistley, Thorpe & Walton Railway, which was sued by its new contractor in 1868 for the £12,000 owed to him for the partially completed works. Judgement was given to Mr Furness and the MT&W was now in deep trouble, its line not yet ready, its capital exhausted, its contractor unpaid, a lien on its assets and the time for completion expired.

By 1869 Captain Jervis had been replaced by the Marquis of Salisbury as chairman, and the latter was to preside over the demise of the unfortunate railway. Abandonment was decided upon at a private meeting of shareholders on 9 July, and a formal application made to the Board of Trade to that end. To satisfy the judgment made in favour of the

The 18.27 service to Colchester standing at Walton-on-the-Naze on 18 August 1993.

contractor, the stocks of sleepers and other materials was sold by auction at the Thorn Inn, Mistley, on 11 and 13 September, but only raised £2,000. Two years later Furness was still trying to clear the debt balance, but the land that the railway had acquired originally now proved virtually worthless. Despite a short period of hope two years later when an East Essex Railway project sought to revive the MT&W line, but with an east-facing connection between Thorpe-le-Soken and Weeley, the unfortunate contractor was destined to remain out of pocket.

The route of the Thorpe, Mistley & Walton railway was to enjoy a brief period of usefulness around 1940 when it was incorpo-rated into a wartime tank ditch, but over the years the physical evidence of the ill-fated project has largely disappeared and today its course is virtually untraceable.

Time has proved that the traffic flow to Clacton, Frinton and Walton is from the London direction and it seems unlikely that the MT&W route would have survived even if it had enjoyed better fortune at the beginning. Where the scheme went wrong it is not easy to say, but this part of Essex is less flat, and construction therefore more difficult and costly, than one might suppose. Furthermore, in addition to picking the wrong contractor, there are other signs that the acumen of the directors fell well short of their enthusiasm.

An empty stock train runs into Thorpe-le-Soken, passing the site where the ill-fated MT&W line would have joined.

20
THE DEFENCE OF
THE TAFF VALE

The *Western Mail* of 17 May 1909 carried a report of the journey of a special train that marked the opening of the Cardiff Railway on the previous Saturday, the 15th. Early in the morning the Marquis of Bute and officials of the Taff Vale Railway had joined the TVR's special saloon and journeyed up the valley to the Bute-Merthyr collieries at Treherbert. After a short stay the saloon was positioned behind the guard's van of a 12-wagon coal train to make a ceremonial return trip to the docks at Cardiff. The newspaper recorded:

'The return journey started at 10.30, and from the Treforest Junction the train proceeded to Cardiff along the new Cardiff Railway to the Bute Docks, this being the first occasion for the line to be traversed. A special engine had been requisitioned, and the engine and train, which were gaily and profusely decorated with flags and festoons, were in the charge of Mr Harland [the Taff Vale's traffic superintendent]. At Pontypridd a salvo of detonators heralded the distinguished party as they passed slowly through the station where Mr O. Hurford, the station master, had made the necessary arrangements.'

It also noted that the coal was passing from the Marquis's own colliery, in his trucks, over his railway and to his docks!

If one was to judge from the report, the whole occasion was a jolly one with the

> **Protagonists:**
> Taff Vale Railway versus
> Bute Dock and allied interests
>
> **Location:**
> South Wales
>
> **Date:**
> 1855-1917

nobleman the honoured guest of the Taff Vale Railway and a whole host of officials and other guests joining in to celebrate the occasion. It hardly seems credible that the railway had been feuding with the Bute docks interests for over half a century, that no more traffic would ever follow the route of the special train and that the junction between the Taff Vale and Cardiff lines at Treforest would be removed in less than six months.

The story behind this event is a long and complex one, running through the whole history of the shipment coal business of South Wales. It is the story of that massive enterprise and of the Taff Vale Railway's defence of its pioneer line against other railways intent on imitating its success or siphoning off some its lucrative business. As it unfolds the story is influenced by the fortunes of the coal industry, themselves reflecting that of the nation and even the empire, and by the seeming injustice of a massive investment in Cardiff docks that earned so poor a return compared with that of the mines and railways they served.

'Winning the coal' - celebrations accompanying the opening of another pit in the Rhondda Valley.

As early as 1767 the issue of transport between the valleys and Cardiff had become important. In that year a fund was established to construct a proper road from Merthyr to the estuary of the Taff River to carry the output of the growing iron industry at the former point. But at this period the modest quays on the lower Taff mainly handled agricultural produce and the population of Cardiff had still to reach the 2,000 figure; there was but little sign of the massive industrial developments ahead. The growth of iron production did lead to the opening of the Glamorganshire Canal in June 1798, but the mining of coal was still confined to meeting the demands of the iron masters. The technology to get at the deeper, richer deposits and produce coal in any quantity had still to be developed.

The growth period for Welsh coal had its beginnings in 1835 when one Thomas Powell began exporting from staiths near the lower end of the Glamorganshire Canal. The year was also significant for the passing of the Taff Vale Railway's Act, although the enterprise was prompted by the iron interests, and the real growth in coal movement was still some 20 years away. In 1839, the year in which the second Marquis of Bute opened what was later to be called Bute West Dock, coal exports were just 6,500 tons!

The outlay on both dock and railway had been considerable, and both parties were anxious to protect their interests. The Taff Vale Railway wanted its own dock outlet and had plans for a harbour at Ely; the Marquis, meanwhile, wanted to encourage all possible traffics and users to his own docks. The two parties held numerous meetings that culminated in an agreement giving the Taff Vale exclusive use of one side of Bute West Dock in return for abandoning the Ely project and the shipments it had been making through its own Little Dock. The first section of the new railway had already been opened, in 1840, and within three years the first simple coal

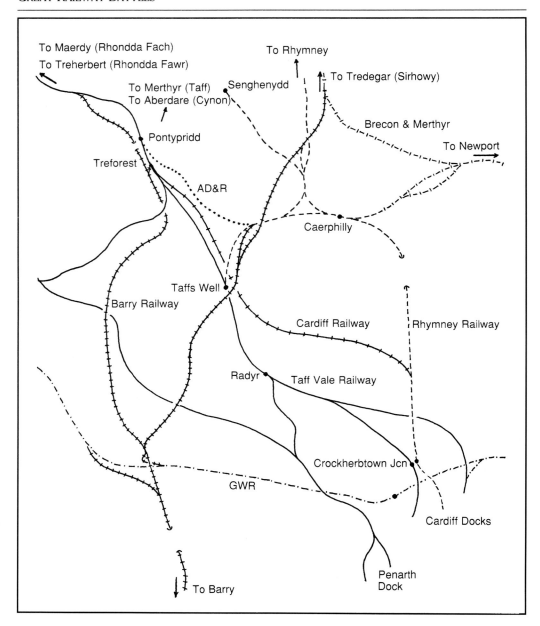

To Maerdy (Rhondda Fach)
To Treherbert (Rhondda Fawr)
To Rhymney
Senghenydd
To Tredegar (Sirhowy)
To Merthyr (Taff)
To Aberdare (Cynon)
Brecon & Merthyr
Pontypridd
To Newport
Treforest
AD&R
Caerphilly
Taffs Well
Barry Railway
Cardiff Railway
Rhymney Railway
Radyr
Taff Vale Railway
Crockherbtown Jcn
GWR
Cardiff Docks
Penarth Dock
To Barry

Pre-Grouping railways in and around Cardiff.

lift had been introduced to supplement barrow transfers between truck and ship.

In 1845 the Marquis of Bute handed over his dock interest to a Trust, and this body took over fully on behalf of the infant heir when the dock-owner died in 1848. This was the first in a chain of events that was to reverse the cordial relationship between railway and dock, although the two did sign a new agreement in 1849. In the following year the South Wales Railway opened and was soon demanding facilities for shipping its coal carryings. The granting of these was accompanied by a decision to build East Bute Dock, and the Taff Vale assumed, in view of its past relationships, that it would be a leading beneficiary.

At this time several of the Bute Trustees held mineral rights in the Rhymney Valley, which, lacking a railway, had yet to develop

beyond iron working and such coal mining as that demanded. Among these men was John Boyle, appointed a Trustee in 1852 and later to become both Managing Trustee for the dock activity and chairman of the Rhymney Railway. He helped to promote the latter to fill the need to provide a line down from the valley to the new dock now under construc-

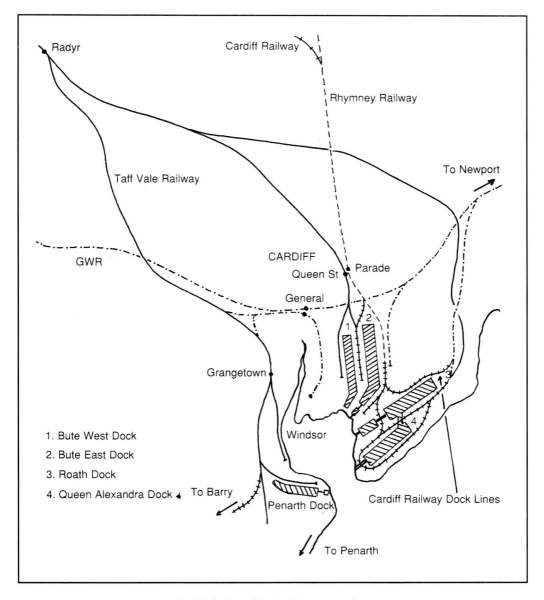

1. Bute West Dock
2. Bute East Dock
3. Roath Dock
4. Queen Alexandra Dock

Cardiff docks and their railway approaches.

tion. The original Rhymney Railway proposals involved using the TVR line south of Llancaiach, but authority for the junction was missing from the Rhymney Railway Act of 24 July 1854. Its amendment of 2 July 1855 put the connection much further south, which involved a significant loss of tolls to the TVR. This factor and the Boyle link between the dock undertaking and Rhymney Railway soon began to undermine the old, comfortable position of the Taff Vale.

The first section of the new East Dock was opened in 1855, a year in which coal exports rose to 1.085 million tons. But the Taff Vale, along with the South Wales Railway, got only three tips at the southern end of the dock, the rest of the space being reserved for the Rhymney company, with only temporary access for the TVR pending its rival's completion. In 1856 Bute Tidal Harbour (later Roath Basin) was opened for coastal shipping, but again was allocated to the upstart Rhymney.

The Taff Vale's response to this situation was to revive the idea of a separate outlet at the mouth of the Ely river. It supported the Ely Tidal Harbour & Railway, which, on 21 July 1856, was incorporated with powers to construct a tidal harbour at Penarth and a railway from there to the TVR main line at Radyr. In the following year the ETH&R became the Penarth Harbour, Dock & Railway, and the Rhymney opened its docks branch - built by and leased to the RR by the docks undertaking! Fully opened in 1858, the Rhymney was then provided with free coal hoists along the east side of Bute East Dock, while the TVR had to pay for its much older ones. The latter was less than happy and stuck an extra 1d per ton on RR traffic exchanged at Crockherbtown to get its own back. Litigation eventually reduced this to 0.8d, but the Taff Vale had made its gesture.

The 1860s brought a fresh round of conflict between the Taff Vale and Rhymney railways. After the latter had been rescued by the dock from financial crisis, the Taff Vale took the Penarth dock company on lease ready for the opening in 1865. The Rhymney then lodged a Bill for its own line from Caerphilly to the docks, a measure that would free it from dependence on the Taff main line section between Walnut Tree and Crockherbtown junctions. The Taff Vale had been having to hand over more than half its coal traffic to the Rhymney because of the latter's stranglehold on the dock unloading facilities, and restricting Rhymney trains over the TV main line south of Walnut Tree had been the only weapon of retaliation. Now, however, the Taff Vale could contest the Rhymney's aspirations in Parliament and was only bought off with the offer of better access to the west side of East Dock.

As the new Rhymney line would relieve the pressure on the Taff Vale main line, the latter company was reasonably pleased with itself, particularly when Penarth Dock opened on 10 June 1865. What was not so pleasing was the Bute Trustees' claim that the TVR lease of the Penarth undertaking was invalid, and that the 1849 agreement precluded the Taff Vale from using an alternative dock without compensation to the Bute coffers. The resultant litigation was to last until 1873, although the Taff Vale won in the end.

In 1866 the warring factions in the Cardiff docks and valleys had to cope with the wider problems of a national financial crisis and a terrible slump in the coal trade. Just nine years later there was another, and by 1878 further major problems were brewing for the Taff Vale. The first developed from a scheme by the Newport interests for a Pontypridd, Caerphilly & Newport Railway that would tap the TVR system south of Pontypridd and siphon off coal that would otherwise have passed to Cardiff. While the PC&N was being built further bombshells went off, first with the launch of the Rhondda & Swansea Bay Railway, then with the lodgement of a Bill for the Barry dock and railway enterprise. At a time when the coal industry itself was changing, with larger companies and higher production, more docks and railways wanted a share of its lucrative transportation business.

Under the weight of these threats, the Taff Vale and Bute negotiators managed to patch up a deal giving the former better Cardiff access. After both the Taff Vale and the

GWR (successor to the South Wales Railway) had reduced their rates to combat the PC&N threat, the former decided that a deal with the Newport line would at least preserve its carryings at the coalfield end. As a result the *Monmouthshire Merlin and South Wales Advertiser* of 4 July 1884 was reporting on a ten-year agreement between the two parties designed to bring semi-anthracite coal down from Rhondda for mixing at Newport with bituminous coal from the Monmouthshire valleys, a process expected to increase the value of both by over 1 shilling a ton. The deal provided for TVR locomotives to work the traffic forward from Pontypridd Junction, over a short Rhymney Railway section at Caerphilly, then on via Brecon & Merthyr metals to Bassaleg. From there GWR tracks of the former Monmouthshire Railway's lines (the so-called Park Mile) were to be used until the connection authorised to the PC&N in 1883 was completed. The new service would move Rhondda coal to Newport for the Cardiff price.

The Great Western, which would be losing business over its main line, did not care for the Taff Vale's solution to its problems one bit. This is dramatically revealed in the newspaper's issue of 11 July, whose entry is paraphrased below:

'On Monday an effort was made to open the Pontypridd, Caerphilly & Newport Railway with a 27-wagon train from Powell Duffryn in the Aberdare Valley. After being stopped at Pontypridd Junction while passenger trains passed, the train moved on to PC&N metals with Mr Hurman of the Taff Vale Railway and other dignitaries on board. The journey went smoothly as far as Bassaleg where the train was brought to an abrupt stand. It was now on the threshold of the Great Western Railway system and Mr Henshaw, the manager of the Brecon & Merthyr line, which the train had traversed from Caerphilly, tendered a permit to the official of the GWR company stationed at this place. He returned it and said he could not allow the train to enter the line of his company. The train was moved to the limit of the boundary and left there, whilst most of the company proceeded to Newport to wait the result of a telegraphic despatch to the head office of the GWR company at Paddington. . .'

In its issue of 1 August the newspaper records the withdrawal of the GWR embargo on the previous Friday and, incidentally, the declaration of 10 per cent dividends by both the Taff Vale and Rhymney concerns, the former with a 6 per cent bonus!

The 1880s and 1890s were dominated by the opening and expansion of the Barry enterprise and by the perennial problems of the Bute Dock Company. With coal traffic still increasing, congestion at Cardiff docks was frequently horrendous. Larger ships were being built to handle bigger loads, but only succeeded in speeding the process of outdating the docks before the last round of investment had started to yield a decent return. While the railways were declaring dividends of 10 per cent on their ordinary shares, the docks capital was yielding less than a 3 per cent return. The solution, it seemed, was to join the transport businesses, and in the years preceding the end of the century the Bute Dock concern sought powers for numerous lines, succeeding with the Cardiff Railway Act of 6 August 1897, which empowered construction of a line from the Rhymney Railway at Heath to a connection with the Taff Vale near Treforest. This would provide a new route for coal, avoiding the lower half of the Taff Vale system and utilising the Rhymney dock access.

The Taff Vale was seriously worried by this new development, which coincided with the rejection of its own Windsor Dock scheme. As work on the Cardiff Railway began, the TVR purchased a strip of land at Treforest that was to prove of immense significance as this latest contest developed. Even at this early stage the Taff Vale Railway was clearly preparing for yet another defence of it system.

In 1902 the Heath-Tongwynlais portion of the Cardiff Railway was completed and negotiations commenced with the TVR for the

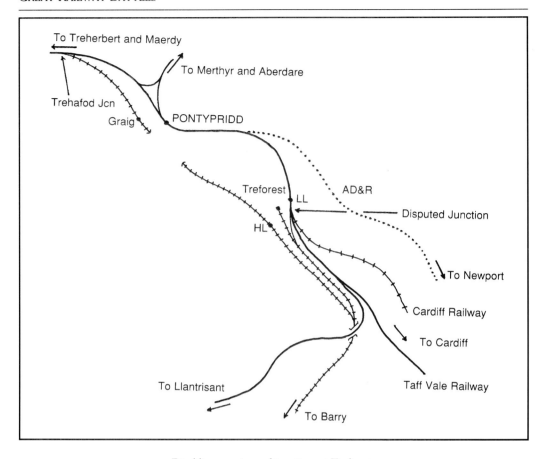

Rival lines, routes and junctions at Treforest.

connection at Treforest. But the latter lost no time in pointing out that the Cardiff Railway's authority was only for a link with the TVR goods lines, and not with the passenger pair, which would need to be crossed to get there. The Cardiff could, if it wanted, have a junction further south, but this would, of course, enable the Taff Vale to retain a higher share of the total rate applying.

Throughout 1903-05 arbitration on this issue was followed by litigation until, in desperation, the Cardiff Railway went again to Parliament for a new Act, which it obtained on 4 August 1906. This seemed to give the dock-inspired enterprise all the powers it needed provided sufficient exchange sidings were put in at the junction, but when the plan for these was forwarded the Taff Vale

again raised objections and another round of arbitration and litigation ensued. The Taff Vale said that it needed the intervening strip of land for its own purposes and raised every possible objection to the layout and adequacy of the proposed exchange sidings.

The intricacies of the dispute over the junction at Treforest tax credulity, but a solution began to seem more likely when negotiations began for a merger of the Taff Vale, Rhymney and Cardiff interests. A Bill was lodged in November 1908 and, as a token of the new-found accord, construction of the disputed connection at Treforest was given the go ahead. As part of the euphoria of the occasion the special train movement described at the beginning of this chapter then took place on 15 May 1909.

The abutments of the bridge, south of Treforest, by which the Cardiff Railway crossed the River Taff, one of the few remains of the ill-fated project.

A northbound 'Valleys' Sprinter leaves Treforest bound for Pontypridd and the Rhondda Valley.

The site of the disputed CR/TVR junction at Treforest.

But the Taff Vale had counted its chickens too early. The opposition by interests at Barry and Newport, who considered the Bute/Cardiff-Taff Vale merger far too threatening, led to the rejection of the fusion Bill on 26 August 1909 and to the TVR reverting to its previous position. By the October instructions had been issued for the removal of the new connection at Treforest, and the whole issue was back where it started.

To salvage something from its massive expenditure, the Cardiff Railway began a passenger service over its truncated railway in 1911. The Marquis now made another ceremonial journey, this time on a steam railcar as far as Rhyd-y-felin, where the route terminated. A public service over the branch was operated from 1 March.

By 1913 coal traffic through Cardiff had reached a record-breaking level of 10.576 million tons. Barry handled slightly more and Newport, Swansea and Penarth were all sharing in the boom from which the Cardiff docks enterprise seemed to be the

only one excluded in terms of making high profits. Determined on another try to obtain access to the coalfield, the Cardiff Railway again approached the Taff Vale for a junction at Treforest. However, that railway had lost so much business to others around the end of the century, and was only just beginning to recover - its 1913 dividend was to be 4 per cent compared with the Barry Railway's 10 per cent - that it was no more ready to be helpful now than when the matter had previously been raised. Again the parties went to law and might, it seems, have been there still had not the influences of war and national unity intervened. These pressures and the approaching retirement of the Taff Vale's general manager eventually resulted in a decision to appoint a single general manager for the three undertakings.

At last there was the opportunity to heal the breach that had begun back in 1855. The Treforest junction issue was dropped by common consent - after all it now no longer mattered which line was used for the vital national coal supplies so long as they got through - and the route lost the importance that had kept it a heated subject in the boardrooms, in the courtrooms and before the arbitrators for so many years.

After the war coal traffic began to decline and, with the Treforest Junction connection no longer needed, the former Cardiff Railway section beyond Rhyd-y-felin was lifted by the Great Western, to whom it now belonged. Today the route carries a 'Valleys' passenger service as far as Coryton, but the junction site at Treforest is now a green field area with only the remains of the approach bridge over the Taff to identify it.

The former Cardiff Railway now ends at these buffers at Coryton.

INDEX